GW00500337

 Pulling~~the~~~~trigger~~

There is recovery and a place beyond. We promise.

 Adam Shaw, a mental illness survivor and mental health advocate, and Lauren Callaghan, an industry-leading clinical psychologist, are the founders of the global mental health publishing enterprise, **Pulling**the**trigger**®. With their TV appearances and global education programmes, Adam, Lauren and their amazing team are helping more people around the world understand, recover from, and talk about their mental health issues.

The **Pulling**the**trigger**® range – user-friendly self-help books with an innovative approach to supporting people recovering from mental health issues.

The**inspirational**series™ – remarkable, real-life stories of men and women who have overcome mental illness to lead fulfilling lives.

Why have we called our books Pullingthetrigger®?

Many things can 'trigger' mental health issues. So what do you do if something makes you feel bad? You stay away from it, right?

I bet you've been avoiding your triggers all your life. But now we know that avoiding them only makes things worse. So here's the game changer: you need to learn how to pull those triggers instead of running away from them – and our **Pulling**the**trigger**® series shows you how. Your recovery is within reach, we promise.

This is more than recovery, it's a way of life.

Adam Shaw & Lauren Callaghan.

First published in Great Britain 2017 by Trigger Press

Trigger Press is a trading style of Shaw Callaghan Ltd & Shaw Callaghan 23 USA, INC.

The Foundation Centre
Navigation House, 48 Millgate, Newark
Nottinghamshire NG24 4TS UK

www.trigger-press.com

British Library Cataloguing in Publication Data

A CIP catalogue record for this book is available upon request
from the British Library

ISBN: 978-1-911246-57-2

This book is also available in the following e-Book formats:

MOBI: 978-1-911246-22-0
EPUB: 978-1-911246-58-9
PDF: 978-1-911246-59-6

Cover design and typeset by Fusion Graphic Design Ltd

Project Management by Out of House Publishing

Printed and bound in Great Britain by TJ International, Padstow

Paper from responsible sources

Theinspirationalseries™
Overcoming adversity and thriving

Searching for Brighter Days
Learning to Manage my Bipolar Brain
By Karen Manton

We are proud to introduce Theinspirationalseries™. Part of the **Pullingthetrigger®** family of innovative self-help mental health books, Theinspirationalseries™ tells the stories of the people who have battled and beaten mental health issues. For more information visit: www.pulling-the-trigger.com

THE AUTHOR

Karen Marie Manton lives in Middlesbrough, North East England. After recently leaving employment with a local authority, she has gone on to write her first non-fiction book: *Searching for Brighter Days*. It follows her transition into adulthood while dealing with a mental illness she didn't know she had. Depicting heartache, loss, and the tribulations of daily life, Karen paints a stark picture of the reality of bipolar disorder.

A strong believer of opening conversations, Karen believes that people need to speak more often about mental health, rather than hiding away. She hopes that by sharing her own story, she can help other sufferers not to feel so alone.

Thank you for purchasing this book.
You are making an incredible difference.

All of The**inspirational**series™ products have substantial
enterprising and philanthropic value and generate proceeds that
contribute towards our global mental health charity,
The Shaw Mind Foundation

MISSION STATEMENT

'We aim to bring to an end the suffering and despair caused
by mental health issues. Our goal is to make help and support
available for every single person in society, from all walks of life.
We will never stop offering hope. These are our promises.'

Pulling the Trigger and The Shaw Mind Foundation

The Shaw Mind Foundation (www.shawmindfoundation.org) offers
unconditional support for all who are affected by mental health
issues. We are a global foundation that is not for profit. Our core
ethos is to help those with mental health issues and their families at
the point of need. We also continue to run and invest in mental health
treatment approaches in local communities around the globe, which
support those from the most vulnerable and socially deprived areas
of society. Please join us and help us make an incredible difference
to those who are suffering with mental health issues. **#lets**do**stuff**.

This is a book for anyone that needs reminding that recovery is possible; you just have to stay in the fight!

Disclaimer: Some names and identifying details have been changed to protect the privacy of individuals.

CHAPTER 1
It's Not Easy Being an Only Child

'Paint me a picture of your childhood,' Eileen, my first community psychiatric nurse (CPN) said.

I assume I must have looked quite taken aback at her question. Nobody had ever asked me to do that before.

At the time, I was feeling quite vulnerable after being discharged from yet another admission to the hospital. I was only 28 years of age, which I considered to be fairly young when you took into account that I'd been suffering with this illness for over 10 years. As I looked at Eileen, I suppose part of me wished that I could be more like her. She'd always appeared to me to be an extremely strong woman, and even in casual clothes she struck quite the figure. I thought she was very attractive, with her long red nails and striking physique. *Yes*, I thought to myself as I sat there, *this is who I want to be, who I could be*. Perhaps at one point in my life I had been a lot stronger – both mentally and physically – but at that point I was so God-damn sensitive. I often found myself overthinking things, to the point where I would worry all day about the smallest of issues.

I began to open up to Eileen, answering her question with memories of my childhood. I told her that I was going to write a book one day, all about my struggles with mental illness. I don't know if she ever took me seriously, but she did tell me that she liked the idea of seeing her name in print one day.

'Oh yes,' I said. 'One day, you will!'

...

It wasn't easy being an only child.

I was brought up in Grangetown, an extremely deprived working-class area in Middlesbrough, in the North East of England. I was born out of wedlock to my parents in 1968, Mary and Kenny, who later married each other. Both of my parents had previous marriages, which meant that they also had other children. Mam had one daughter, Susan, while Dad had four: Michael, Kathleen, Kevin, and Pauline. Mam always said that she 'went in for me' when I was born, that she had planned to have a baby and was glad it turned out to be me, like she'd been waiting on a list for a council house.

However, despite having so many siblings, I was a bit of a loner growing up. It often seemed that they felt a touch of resentment towards me, as they all only had one parent while I had both. There were many times during my childhood when I wish my parents had broken up as well, so that I could be somewhat like my brothers and sisters. The saying 'an only child is a lonely child' rang true for me during my entire childhood.

One of my earliest memories is of me being in my parent's bedroom, lying in my cot, and having a tantrum because all I wanted was to be in their bed. But they never let me. And so alone I stayed.

At the tender age of four, I left the house alone in the dead of night. My parents have told me this story many times, though I don't remember it myself. According to them, I took myself to the local bus stop and waited there. Fortunately for me, a police officer walked up to me and asked what I was doing. So I told him that I was waiting for Dad, who worked on the dredgers. The police officer then carried me into The Gem, the nearby newsagent shop, and asked if anyone there knew where I lived. Apparently they all noted how well-dressed I was in my pyjamas, with my dressing gown wrapped around me and my slippers on. Thankfully one of them knew where I lived and I was taken home, where Mam was screaming like a banshee at the sight of the police officer.

Ironically, it turned out that Dad wasn't even at work. He'd been upstairs the entire time, fast asleep. Despite all the things that I went through in regards to my father, I truly did love him. So much so that I was willing to wait in the cold night for him!

I think it's safe to say that I was a complete and utter daddy's girl. My love for him was crystal clear for everyone to see. As soon as Dad came home from work, I would always want him to play, whether it be 'catchies' with the ball (a name that we used for passing it back to one another without dropping it), playing snap with playing cards, or simply tickling me till my sides ached. As long as I had his time, that was all that mattered. I loved it when he made my big stuffed panda bear talk; I could sit watching him do that all night. I hung onto every word he said; no matter what Mam told me, I would always want to know what Dad thought of something. Once I became really distressed at a visit to the dentist, and even though Mam was there to hold my hand I was still screaming for Dad.

Every morning, Dad would wake up early, no matter what. And in the cold winter months, he would always make sure that there was a blazing fire lit for me and Mam when we came downstairs. Mam would always go straight to the kitchen and make porridge for us, which was a very welcome sight on a cold morning!

I can picture every single detail of our home. It was a very cold house, as we didn't have any central heating. The fire in the living room was the only source of heat in the entire place. It was meant to be a coke fire, but Dad removed the door from it and made it a coal fire because coke was too expensive for us to buy. The coal was kept in a bunker at the back of the garden, which, at the time, I thought was a huge jungle! The grass in the garden was about four feet high and seemed to stretch on for miles and miles. All the children would use it as a shortcut to the ICI fields, the local works company. Mam and Dad reckoned that it had been like that since day one, and had attempted to sort it out on occasion, but had never made much progress. I think that they felt as though they were fighting a losing battle, so they never really tried that hard to keep it neat.

In the downstairs of the house, we had a living room, a back kitchen (as it was called in those days) with a cooker, an old-fashioned washing machine that had a wringer on it, and a little bathroom leading off the kitchen. There wasn't a toilet there though. That was in a small shed-like room next door. I hated having to rush out in the night whenever nature called! Upstairs, there were two large bedrooms: one for my parents, and one for me.

Looking at our house, you might have guessed that we were fairly poor, but I have to say, as a child I was well looked after. I never went short of anything. Mam and Dad always made sure that there was food on the table, and I was always well dressed. Dad was a grafter; he worked as a rigger and tried his best to ensure that he always had a job. This wasn't an easy task and Mam often described it as 'living in a feast or a famine'. So, to help out, she had a few cleaning jobs on the go. I know that it was often difficult for them to make ends meet. There was many a time when Mam would have to go and see my nana Lizzie to 'have a borrow' to get by, especially when Dad was between contracts. But despite these lean times, I still felt as though the majority of my childhood was filled with happy times.

I can still see, in my mind's eye, all the dollies in my bedroom with their prams, cots, and all the other bits and bobs. I always knew I wanted to be a mammy, from a very young age. I was lucky in that I had a massive bedroom; it may have been bitterly cold but was great for playing. I would sit for hours just preening my dolls, combing their hair, and putting them in lovely clothes. I would then wrap them in their blankets and put them in the pram ready for their trip out. I was constantly playing with all my toys, and being on my own for so long meant that a good imagination was a necessity.

These pre-school years were mostly spent with Mam. Nursery wasn't compulsory, so Mam made the decision for me to stay at home with her. I spent most of my days helping her around the house ... Well, as much as a toddler could help anyway. I'm pretty sure I came across as more of a hindrance as I got busy with the feather duster and broke lots of small items in the process.

Looking back now, I'm sure that it would have made a lot more sense for me to go to nursery, especially because I didn't have any brothers or sisters to play with and I was too young to be playing outside. But I realise now that it was more for Mam's benefit than mine. She had a need for me to be around her, and I understand now that that was because she felt lonely all the time, what with Dad never really being around. She became dependent on me, and I don't think that ever passed.

Finally, the day arrived for me to begin school. Even as a young kid I felt guilty about leaving Mam all alone in this big house in order to go to school. But I did always feel happy when I came home. As time went on, I soon formed my own circle of friends and we were to stick together for some time to come. There was Susan, Janine, Mark (Fitzy), Jeannette, and Katherine. Having friends was a brand-new experience and they meant so much to me. We had so many laughs together at the old infant school, which was ruled by the iron rod of Sister Apoline. She was a nun who was definitely not to be messed with.

There are so many memories that flash to mind. Mostly of dinnertime. This time of day became a total nightmare for me, as I struggled with the meals I was given. We would all sit at a table for five, and a teacher would serve the meals. They would always ask us if we wanted 'half or whole'. I remember feeling sick in the pit of my stomach as I looked at the tureens full of the usual school dinner slop. I would timidly say 'Half, please' and most of the time, I would get what I asked for. But I can remember one occasion where I had Mrs Locket, a teacher who was well-known for putting the fear of God into any child. When I asked her for half, she whacked great dollops of food onto my plate. Looking at the large mound of it, I instantly felt my stomach churn. Looking at the plate was enough to make me feel ill. As I started to eat a mouthful of peas, I felt my stomach twinge. My friends all knew the signs.

'Miss, Karen's going to be sick,' one of them blurted out.

Mrs Locket glared at me and her face went red as she yelled at me, 'Go to the toilet!'

I ran as fast as my little legs could carry me and I just about made it to the toilet. There were tears streaming down my face. And if that wasn't enough, things were about to get even worse. As I turned away from the toilet to unlock the latch on the door, I found that it wouldn't budge. It dawned on me that I was locked in.

I started to bang on the door for what seemed to me like an eternity, trapped in that cubicle. Thankfully, Miss Waterfield arrived. 'Miss, let me out!' I yelled. 'I'm stuck in the toilet!'

Just as I shouted, I heard another voice that cut through me like a knife. *Oh no*, I thought, *it's Sister Apoline*. She was demanding to know what all the commotion was about. I could hear Miss Waterfield explaining and almost fell on the floor when I heard Sister Apoline reply, 'Just leave her there'. My face must have been a picture of pure terror. But thankfully Miss Waterfield would never have done that to me, and managed to climb up and put her hand over the door to unlock the latch. *Phew!* I thought. *That was close*. I kept quiet for the rest of the day, but almost broke my neck when I got home in the rush to tell Mam of the day's events.

Mam was furious to say the least and penned a letter to the school, telling them that in future I was to sit on my teacher Mrs Murray's table. She was a gentle kind soul. The letter was handed in to Sister Apoline and it wasn't long before I was summoned to her office. 'What is the meaning of this?' She was waving the letter frantically in the air, furious about it. 'What would I do if 33 children wanted to sit at Mrs Murray's table?'

I wanted to tell her she should maybe get a really big table, but looking at her face, I decided it was not the best way forward.

'In future, you will sit at my table, child,' she said. Definitely not the outcome I was hoping for. The only good thing to come from this was that at least she listened to me and ensured I did only receive small portions of dinner!

When I think back to what those poor teachers had to contend with ... I certainly wasn't the easiest of pupils. One morning I left for school knowing full well that I wasn't going to even enter the school gates. Don't get me wrong, I loved school. But not this day, because this was the day that we were going to have to draw a bus. That's right, a bus. And this terrified me for reasons that I'm not entirely sure about. Looking back now, I think maybe it was because I wasn't creative at all, and I was so scared of getting it wrong. I was such a perfectionist, even then. It seems so bizarre to me now, but the idea of drawing something that had so many bits to it, so many details, so many chances for me to make mistakes, made me want to cry. I just didn't want to appear stupid to my friends.

I tossed and turned all night over the prospect of drawing this bus, and when I neared the school gate in the morning, I ran. I don't think Mam could believe what was happening. My favourite teacher, Miss Short, tried so hard to reassure me. 'What's wrong, Karen?' she yelled after me. 'You normally love school!'

'Well, not today!' I shouted back, and shot off along the road, followed closely by Mam and a woman we called Nitnue. She was a tall, thin lady, with blonde hair that stuck all the way up. We called her this because she was often teased and would shout 'I'll hit you' to the people who bothered her, but she had trouble pronouncing the words properly. Mam shouted at me angrily, and maybe she thought this would scare me into stopping, but it only made me go faster. I could feel her getting ever closer, so I ran and ran. I eventually saw that green door, the door to my house, and threw myself in, collapsing on the sofa.

Dad just stared at me, waiting for me to explain what had happened. He didn't have to wait too long, because Mam was right behind me and not too happy.

Annoyingly, I returned to school the next day to find that the art lesson had been cancelled and that I had to draw the big red bus on that day instead. My friends all thought it was hilarious, and I became the talk of the playground for a little while. This didn't harm our friendships, though: we only became closer as time went by.

Although I can paint a lovely picture in my head when I think about my childhood, sadly that wasn't always the case. I can recall a lot more about being such a young, tender age than I should be able to and some memories will haunt me forever. I saw far too many things that children should be protected from. And because of this, my love for Dad was soon replaced with resentment and abject fear.

As Dad was such a hard worker, he coped by becoming an even heavier drinker. Every night, if he had money in his pocket, he would head to the boozer. This led to a lot of arguments and violence. You see, as Dad went out drinking a lot, Mam wanted to try to keep up with him some of the time. As I was the only child living at home, I often felt as though I was an inconvenience to both of them. In order for Mam to go out of an evening with Dad, there needed to be some sort of provision in place for me. Sometimes she would send me to my nana Lizzie or ask a woman a few doors down to pop in and check on me from time to time. With her wrinkly face and a big wart on the end of her nose, she looked like a witch! But she always checked on me, and always made sure that I was safe.

I remember a time when my parents were arguing in the kitchen. Though I use the word argument, it was really more Dad shouting at Mam, not letting her say anything. I felt helpless as I stood there, watching her cry buckets, his voice getting louder and louder. I can remember Susan, Mam's other daughter who would sometimes spend time in our house, scooping me up in her arms and taking me on a bus late at night to the safety of my nana Lizzie, my mam's mother. She lived in South Bank, about three miles away. I'm glad Susan was around to take me away from all the upset that day.

Many arguments would start at tea-time, when Dad, full of drink, would realise that his tea wasn't good enough. He would scream and shout and sometimes even throw his plate at the wall. Poor Mam, terrified and vulnerable, would often grab me and run out of the house to Nana Lizzie's. But, much to my terror, we would always go back when things blew over.

Nana Lizzie often told Mam to leave Dad, for her own safety and mine, but Mam wouldn't hear of it. And so the arguments continued and, sadly, so did the violence. The violence always followed on from the long hours in the boozer. Mam didn't have to say anything too incendiary. She'd only need to make one small comment and Dad would take it the wrong way. He would then slap her hard around the face. He'd also slap her if she didn't manage to get any supper prepared for him. I'll never understand why she stayed and put up with it all.

One Christmas, when I was around nine years of age, Mam and Dad decided to have a house party and invite some of their friends round. I was very excited as I was allowed to sit with all the grownups. Everyone appeared to be having a lovely night and laughter filled the home. I enjoyed just sitting and listening to all their stories and hearing their singing. It was such a fun night, but all of a sudden it transformed into one of the worst memories from my childhood.

Everyone had left for their own homes, the night drawing to a close. Mam, like everyone else, had enjoyed a few drinks. It wasn't that she was a big drinker – not like Dad – but she had mixed her drinks a little and a few gin and oranges had made her feel ill. She had gone upstairs to bed, feeling poorly, and had ended up throwing up. And so Dad decided to join her upstairs. I followed suit.

I can still remember him yelling at her and dragging her around the bedroom. I screamed at him to stop. Mam was lying on a green and white shag pile rug and Dad was kicking her violently, trying to make her get up. I screamed with every impact. The sight of the violence was unbearable and I felt so helpless just standing there, unable to do anything. I just yelled and cried but Dad didn't pay any attention to me. Eventually, when it was safe, I rushed to Mam's aid. It was just sickening; there were no other words to describe his disgusting actions. That night, like so many others, Mam and I held each other as she slept in my bed, both trying to hide our silent tears.

The next morning everything was so calm and different. Dad made Mam her usual morning cuppa as though nothing had happened. But this time Mam wouldn't speak to him. Instead, they undertook their conversation through me. It really was a terrible atmosphere in the room as I just looked at Dad, struggling to believe this was the same person as the vile animal I had watched last night.

Around this time the movie *Grease* had just come to the cinema in town and Mam decided that she would take me to see it. It was an outing for the two of us, but would also keep her out of Dad's way, to punish him for what he had put her through. I jumped at the chance, as this was a lovely opportunity to spend some quality time with Mam. We had a lovely afternoon, enjoying chocolates and watching a fantastic film. Throughout the day, though, I kept scrutinising her, unable to forget the horrific images of the night before. She didn't deserve to be hurt in that way.

Mam was a lovely, kind person, who always tried to do the best for us. Perhaps she didn't always get things right, but what parent ever does? She tried so hard to make sure that I never wanted for anything, to give me nice clothes and toys, to make me feel loved.

We loved each other fiercely. And I suppose sometimes our roles shifted and I would play the mother for her. I wanted to protect her from my father as much as I could, but because I was so young, there was little that I could do. I can remember threatening my dad with a knife at one point, a very frightening thing for a child to do. At that point, I felt that there was nothing else I could do. Even then I wanted Dad to go away as I knew that Mam would be happy then. She was always so happy before he came back from work or after his nights of drinking, and then the tide would change. So many nights I cried myself to sleep, horrific and distressing images of violence playing themselves out in my mind.

By this point, I'd become close friends with the kids who lived on the same road as me, and soon I learnt that my parents' behaviour wasn't unusual. That was somewhat of a relief, but it did make us all feel very sad. There was some comfort in knowing that I was not alone, and that my friends knew how I was feeling. But it was hardly a good club to be a part of! I had a few friends whose fathers also liked to drink too much and who had also seen domestic violence on far too many occasions. I think that's why we all really stuck together, and had a strong bond with one another. I also realised that the children weren't the only ones who discussed each other's homes. What happened behind our closed doors was also very difficult to hide from the adults down our street, and we soon became the subject of gossip between those whose daily lives were less dramatic. This upset Mam to no end.

I remember loving the endless summer nights playing out in our road with the other children. As long as we had a pair of skipping ropes we didn't want the night to end! We would stretch the rope from one end of the path to the other and play under the moon all night long. We kept ourselves busy with games such as Bulldog, My Eye, Stuck in the Mud, and so on. I remember getting together a few close friends and telling them that we were 'the Sunshine gang'. I'm not entirely sure what it meant but off we would all head over the fields of the ICI just at the foot of our garden to kick a ball or climb the trees, often heading to the beck where we knew we were pushing our luck and there we would play until the night started to draw in. There was something about those days that could never be the same now. We were filled with the innocence of youth. There was this feeling of safety that cannot be said about life today. I would never have swapped those childhood days for anything.

When I went out playing with my friends, I was like a caged animal being let loose. Playing became an outlet; it allowed me to become a normal child for a while and not a child who carried the weight of all the burdens from home on her shoulders. The state of our home life depended on Dad and what mood he was in when returning from the boozer. Honestly, it was like walking on eggshells. We always felt so tense and my nerves were shot for a lot of the time.

Often it was more peaceful if he had no work or if he was between contracts, because no work meant no beer money. We did struggle financially when this happened but we were very careful with the pennies and Mam always ensured that we all had good food to eat. We managed to 'get by', as she described it. Secretly I think she preferred having to struggle a little with money rather than face the alternative.

Dad often visited his mum, my nana Maisie. Nana Maisie was a very different person to Dad. She was so angelic and one of the loveliest people you could ask to meet. She didn't drink, swear, or speak ill of anyone. Unfortunately, she didn't live a peaceful life either. One of her sons, Uncle Barry, lived at home with her and also enjoyed the 'demon drink'. He made his home brew, and Dad was often partial to a pint or two of it. It was a very heavy drink and was nicknamed the 'slamming door gear', which I think was pretty self-explanatory. My nana often wondered how she could have had three sons (Kenny, Barry, and Desi) who all enjoyed more than their fair share of drink when she herself would never touch alcohol. I guess seeing the downside of it, as she often did, would be enough to put anyone off.

I loved going to see Nana. She was just so sweet. I would often walk the long roads with Dad to get to her house, and back then the roads seemed never-ending. Dad would often tell me to take my nail polish off before going, because Nana wouldn't like it. She was fairly strict, but never quite as strict with me as she was with the others. I think she knew that I was a little rebel anyway.

But despite how strict she was, Nana would never call her sons out for their behaviour. She never believed they could do anything wrong. She chose to bury her head in the sand, quite frankly, and on the odd occasion Mam confided in her about Dad's behaviour she would advise Mam to walk out of the house until he had cooled off. She never really got involved in their domestic situation.

Perhaps she, like others, just preferred to believe it wasn't happening.

CHAPTER 2

My World in One Word: Grangetown

As much as I enjoyed my stays with Nana Maisie, I had to be careful not to upset my other nana, Nana Lizzie. Both nanas enjoyed my company but I always felt that I should never choose one over the other. For that reason I tried to share my affections between them as equally as possible. Nana Lizzie, my mam's mam, tended to get a little bit jealous from time to time if I talked too much about Maisie. Both my granddads passed away when I was very young, but I got so much love from my nanas. Nana Lizzie was a very big part of my life and I was with her for an awful lot of my childhood. She too was a very special lady but very different in many ways to my other nana.

Sadly, Nana Lizzie only had one surviving child: my mam, Mary. She always told me that she did have more babies but back then times were very hard and they had all died soon after they were born. I'm not really sure of the cause but from what Nana would tell me it sounded as though it was perhaps down to malnutrition. I never pressed her for answers, because I knew that it would upset her deeply and I never wanted to do that. She was good at putting on a brave face most of the time, but talking about her babies who had died always, understandably, made her cry.

I was only very young when Nana came to live in Grangetown around the corner from where we lived. It was literally only doors away, on St George's Road. This was very handy for Mam as she had an escape route for when things became heated between her and Dad. One time she turned up on Nana's doorstep with a big pan of stew in her hand. Dad had screamed at her, telling her that the food was 'a lot of fucking rubbish.' It's interesting to think about this as an adult. Mam was so upset, but I think I would have been incredibly angry if it was done to me. I don't know how he dared to say anything like that. He would never get away with saying something like that to me now!

This became the regular thing for some time: Mam running to Nana upset, and Nana Lizzie begging her to leave. Of course, the fact that she stayed caused a lot of resentment between Nana and Dad. There was a time when Nana really disliked him. In fact, I think dislike was an understatement. I'm pretty sure she hated him.

My half-sister Susan was very close to Nana Lizzie as Nana helped to raise her. Susan was a teenager when Mam and Dad met and as far as I'm aware Mam and Susan's father decided that, as she was very close to Nana, it would be better if she lived with her. Susan was quite a headstrong, determined teenager and quite rebellious at times, and I think this made life hard for Nana. They were very close though.

Susan got pregnant at a very young age. As it happened there were only three years of difference between me and her our John, so we virtually grew up together. Looking back, I suppose that John became the brother I never had. He would always spend a lot of time at Nana Lizzie's, and we spent many happy times there together. We had great fun fighting over Nana's ginger tom cat, Micky, both of us desperate to be the one to cuddle him. Often Micky would run off into the garden to get away from the two of us, which we found hilarious, to be honest!

Only a few years later Susan had another boy with her new chap Glenn. As a family we were thrilled, and we all doted on Glenn Jr, or 'little Glenn' as we called him. This was great as I knew this would be another playmate for John and me. I was looking forward to the day when he was a bit older and we could all hang out together. Having family around me that made me feel good really helped me, considering how miserable I felt around Dad all the time. I needed that. I craved love and affection at a time where violence was almost the norm.

Changes also started happening in the area that I was growing up in. When I was around eight or nine, the council decided to demolish our house. Nana Lizzie's, too. I felt a deep sense of loss and sorrow when Mam told me that we had to leave our house. I'd always thought that we were going to live there forever and now it felt like I was having a rug pulled from underneath me. Life was so hectic and traumatic as it was: could I really handle such a big upheaval? The sick feeling in my stomach suggested that perhaps I couldn't.

Mam and Dad were given the option of moving to a house quite far away, in a place called Normanby, or moving to the other end of the road where some remaining houses were being modernised. For my parents, it was a no-brainer: there was no way they were going to leave their beloved Grangetown. And so they chose to accept the offer of moving into number five as soon as it was ready. I suppose, looking back, that it was lovely in comparison to the old house, although my emotions at the time were never so simple. We finally had a bathroom upstairs, though, which included a toilet. An inside toilet. What a luxury! My bedroom was a lot smaller than my old one – merely a box bedroom – but Mam reassured me that she would make it perfect for me. That helped calm my nerves and helped get me through my fear of change.

On the morning of the move, Mam told me that when I came home from school to go straight to the new house as we would be living there from now on. I felt quite excited by then, as most of my friends had all moved to their new houses as well and it felt like a shared adventure.

I wasn't disappointed, as it did look so nice. Mam had been busy having carpets and new curtains fitted. There was also some really nice new furniture. I couldn't wait to see my new room! I rushed upstairs and the first thing I noticed was how warm and cosy it was. Of course, this new modernised house had central heating, which meant that a radiator was in every room. It was a first for us! Mam had put up some new striped thick curtains for me, which were quite trendy at the time. My window was double-glazed and even had a blind over it. All of these had been fitted in by the council, as we were quite near to the main road and they hoped that it would reduce some of the noise level. There was also a brand-new single bed and wardrobe. I felt so happy with my new room, and couldn't wait for bedtime! Something about it made me feel safe and protected, in a way that the old house never had.

Mam had taken on a little cleaning job by this point. Her friends would call to the house for her and have a quick cuppa before setting off for work at 4.30pm. Work was just a walk up the road then a lift into ICI Wilton, where they worked as cleaners in the medical block. It was only for a couple of hours and Mam would return home at about 7pm. The pay wasn't great but I think Mam enjoyed spending some time with her friends. It helped take her mind off the horrors of her domestic abuse and the stress of constant arguing, which was really beginning to grind her down. She was very happy showing her friends our new home. I could see Mam felt really proud of this place, and for the first time ever she actually had a lovely garden and was able to make plans for what she wanted for the rear garden.

The new place felt luxurious and suddenly we were experiencing a whole new standard of living. My anxiety levels lowered and I felt a bit silly for how I'd reacted to the news. Whenever Mam went off to work, I hurried off to play in my new room. I would sit at my desk and pretend to have a classroom full of children. I would hand out exercise books to my imaginary pupils and teach using my blackboard. I would talk away to my class but become very quiet when Dad came home because I didn't want him to hear me talking to myself! His temper was unpredictable at the best of times.

Slowly but surely, my school life changed as well. I loved primary school; it was definitely my favourite as my most positive experiences happened there. Ours was a very old school, typical of its era with long brick corridors and red brick floors. The classrooms had very high ceilings with old desks and chairs. Dad had gone to this school and it was nicknamed 'the old farm school'. The teachers had been fantastic too, each and every one of them. At break time and lunchtime, the teacher would select a pupil to walk the length of the corridor and ring the old hand bell. I found that the school had a charm to it that these modern-day schools now lack.

One of the happiest years for me had been second year. My teacher was Mr Wafer, and he was really quite cool. Everyone looked forward to the end of the afternoon when lessons were almost over and he would read *Charlie and the Chocolate Factory* to us. He made every part of the book sound so dramatic and real. We knew we had to be on our best behaviour for this to happen as this was a treat for us. Besides, if we were not on our best behaviour, chalk would come flying across the classroom or some of the really naughty boys were threatened with a slipper!

One day Mr Wafer had advised me, on my school report, to visit the library in the school holidays. He thought it would help me with my reading and increase my confidence. I did just that and it had a big impact on me. As a result I was often chosen to be the narrator for the school plays. We really respected teachers back then, and we all turned out to be very clever little kids.

But seemingly very quickly, the final year was upon us. As I got older my relationships with the other kids in my area became a bit more fragile. We were heading towards the end of primary school and our groups started to split up. I think it was a combination of finding new friends and knowing we were about to embrace the senior school where things were going to be very different. I found this really hard to accept at a time where my home life was changing so rapidly. Nothing felt stable or familiar any more and I hated it. I wanted to freeze time and stay in this school forever.

Change has always bothered me. Teachers from senior school came and talked to us to prepare us for what was to come, but I still didn't feel ready. On our last day, I met Mam at the shops after school, tears streaming down my face. This was my first experience of the heartache of growing up.

The next hurdle for me to climb was facing the prospect of starting senior school. I had already been through so much emotional turmoil. How was I going to handle this?

CHAPTER 3

No Longer Just a Child

Starting senior school was particularly hard for me, because we'd gone on holiday to Wallis' in Cayton Bay, Scarborough, for the school holidays and we got back a few days later than everyone else. Although it had been great having a few extra days off school to go on holiday, it had put me at a real disadvantage to the other children because it meant that I was starting senior school all on my own. All the other pupils had already had a few days to get used to everything and to get to know one another. This made an already nerve-wracking day incredibly daunting!

Unfortunately, it was all eyes on me as I was the new kid on the block. And if this wasn't enough, there was a whole other reason why I stuck out. Mam had obeyed the rules to the letter, which was why I turned up in full school uniform on the first day: a long, navy pleated skirt, white shirt, tie, and a black blazer with new school shoes. I thought I looked like the most perfect student ever. My bubble was very quickly burst, though, and I was horrified to see that I was in a minority as the rest of the girls were wearing red or navy-checked open shirts. I felt like a right idiot.

The form classes had already been arranged by the time I started, so I was told that I was in 1PL. On arriving at the classroom, I desperately looked around for some of my old school friends and though there were a few of them, they weren't really the ones that I had hung around with in junior school. There were a lot of new faces. Now the class was full of pupils from the surrounding three junior schools and there were quite a few of us.

And it didn't seem that it was going well. I had no sooner joined the line waiting outside the classroom door when someone dared me to call a lad by his nickname, which I mistakenly thought he wouldn't have minded. I was soon to be proved wrong when he marched over to me and gave me a good kick. Tears welled up in my eyes as I struggled to compute what had just happened. What a great start to the day!

The teacher arrived, and he seemed like a real canny chap. The register was then called and I was given my timetable. It all seemed a bit alien to me and would take some getting used to. I did wish that I hadn't gone on that holiday and started with everyone else, as that first day was very scary and I felt so alone trying to stand on my own two feet.

Lunchtime was a little scary as it seemed to be that a few lasses wanted to make their presence noticed. I was stood in the dinner queue when a girl spun round and accused me of staring at her. *Oh, God*. I thought. *Here we go*. Luckily for me, she just gave me a look and swung back round, but the damage was done. I felt so vulnerable and on edge for the rest of day – it was exactly like being at home around Dad.

I managed to make some new friends and had the odd chat with an old friend here and there, but other than that I felt isolated. I think things would have been so much easier if the school bullies hadn't noticed me early on and decided to target me on the school bus going home.

I have vivid memories of one girl, who seemed a fair bit older than me and who I had never seen before, coming up to me on the bus home and squirting tomato ketchup all over my hair and clothes.

I was absolutely mortified. How could someone dislike me so much to do that to me, without even knowing who I was? Was it the uniform? Had I made myself a target? I fought hard to blink back the tears as I walked home, ignoring the crowd of girls who cheered her on and laughed. Kids were so cruel even back then.

I couldn't get home fast enough. It was almost comedic in a kind of tragic way when, as I walked into the kitchen, Mam asked, 'Karen, do you want red or brown sauce on your tea?'

'I think I've had enough sauce to last a lifetime,' I replied as I entered the kitchen.

An expression of pure fury appeared on Mam's face when it dawned on her what had happened to me. She started shouting and screaming, demanding to know who this girl was. When I explained that it had happened on the school bus, I knew what would happen next. She would do whatever she could to protect me. Mam would always have my back; she would never stand for anyone abusing me. Now that I think about it I think that was her way, psychologically, of retaliating against the crap that Dad had put her through her entire life. Maybe she felt strong when she stood up for me but, sadly, she could never stand up for herself. Oddly enough, Dad was always proud of how she defended her family. Though he was angry about what had happened to me, he left it to Mam to decide what to do.

The next morning, Mam set off with me as I headed for the school bus. This wasn't too strange as the bus stop was on her way to work. What was strange was when Mam got onto the bus with me. I couldn't believe what was happening but considering the mood Mam was in, I thought it was best to just keep quiet. She said something to the driver and then marched to the back of the bus towards the girl who had squirted ketchup all over me. I hurried off upstairs but could see what was happening in the mirror. I watched as Mam grabbed the girl by the collar, demanding to know what the hell she thought she was playing at.

'Don't you ever do that to my daughter again!' Mam yelled at her.

The girl went bright red as Mam continued to shout at her and warn her against bullying me again. Mam then retreated off the bus and left me feeling incredibly nervous. Everyone just looked on in silent amazement at what had just taken place. Anxiety gripped at my heart. What would be the consequences of what Mam had just done? What if it made matters worse?

Thankfully, there were no repercussions of the sauce episode at school. Surprisingly, my school friends had nothing but praise for Mam. But it was a different story come the evening.

That night there was a knock at our front door. It was no surprise to see Jennifer (as we learnt was the girl's name) standing with her parents on our doorstep, ready to do battle with Mam. There was plenty of talking done but they were quite reasonable when Mam explained why she had been so upset and angry. Of course, Dad was there too to back us up, but he didn't say much. Thankfully, everything ended quite amicably and Jennifer was told to apologise for what she had done to me. I was so relieved at the outcome, but it did put me on a constant knife edge, scared of anything similar happening again.

Following on from this incident things improved at school. I soon made new friends and began to let go of the past. Eventually I found myself enjoying it and looking forward to attending every day. I started to hang out with a new friend named Christine and we became really good mates. We would spend lots of time at one another's houses, just like I did with my old friends. This helped soothe my anxiety, as once again I felt myself feeling more safe and secure than I had for a while.

The first year seemed to fly by and we were soon heading off on our annual school trip, to Scarborough of all places, just before we broke up for school holidays. By this point I had developed a crush on my form teacher, the poor man, and was delighted when he announced he was to be my form teacher for the next five years.

I didn't see anything wrong with my crush; I was sure lots of girls developed crushes on their teachers. I couldn't get enough of mine, and admittedly he made school fun for me. As a result, school became a really positive experience for me and I was so happy when my school report showed some very good test results and a hundred per cent attendance record. My parents were so pleased that I really seemed to love school.

The fun was really going to start now, though, now that school was over, because the start of the school holidays meant only one thing: the countdown to our next holiday at Wallis'. This year was going to be a little different as Mam felt that it was time for me to be going into the grown-up club with her and Nana Lizzie. The fact that I was only coming up to age thirteen seemed irrelevant to Mam. She told me she'd order my pass for me because I looked older than thirteen and it wouldn't be a problem. It has to be said that I was a very mature thirteen-year-old.

Mam had booked us into the motel this time, rather than the caravan we had the first time around, so we felt really posh. It had a lovely bar attached to the side, which was run by a really sweet older gentleman. I'm sure Nana had taken a shine to him. The motel also had its own two private outdoor pools, which were absolutely freezing. I only braved them once or twice. It was lovely to stand out on the balcony at night looking over at the pools which were covered with netting but still glistened in the moonlight. The large white Club Rendezvous had beautiful flowers outside, which were all lit up. It really did look amazing all put together like that.

Needless to say, I was only drinking soft drinks but that didn't stop me having a fabulous time. I just loved the entertainment and it gave me a real buzz. It was so much more sophisticated than the shows they put on for kids my age and I was drawn to that. Dressing up older than my years gave me a confidence boost and my self-esteem levels rose ever higher as I walked around looking smarter than I ever had before.

Once again, the holiday came to an end all too soon. I fell back down to earth with a bump and school was a kind of harsh reality. I still enjoyed school and continued to try my hardest, but I did feel different from my classmates, like I'd experienced a part of life that they hadn't. In fact, that was the situation for both my second and third year as well. More holidays at Wallis' followed and with each passing year I felt my attitude and tastes change. I didn't feel like a little kid any more. I wanted to be something more.

Most people noticed and acknowledged that I was very mature for my age, and I did dress more maturely too. I'm not sure if it was because I was an only child or because my childhood hadn't been brilliant, but all of a sudden I decided I just wanted to be in the adult world. It became a need and a driving force behind everything I did.

On reflection, I can now see that encouraging this behaviour wasn't the smartest move Mam had ever made. But then again, I was becoming rebellious, much like my sister Susan. Maybe Mam felt that she never had an option. Although I was a very loving, caring daughter who would have done anything for my parents, I was also very headstrong and I know that at times I was more than a handful.

As I hurtled towards my fourteenth birthday, I became aware of my growing feelings towards men, and I developed one crush after another. It would always be either someone from the TV or a teacher from school. I suppose this is normal for any young girl but my crushes always seemed to be for older men. I still don't really know why I could never form a romantic attachment with someone my age, or even close to it. Nevertheless, rightly or wrongly Mam was aware of my growing maturity and therefore by the time I was fifteen she was taking me with her to the local club once a week. Dad wasn't happy about this, but Mam sold the idea to him by convincing him that it was better that they knew where I was.

For quite a long time this worked really well, and then I started bringing a friend of mine with us. She was a little older than me but we got on well. It goes without saying that I only ever drank bitter lemon but it was the company and the music that I really enjoyed. Mam had started giving me the child benefit money that she received for me, and I took the opportunity to buy new dresses through my nana's catalogue. Needless to say, I bought the most grown-up outfits and high-heeled shoes I could find, ones that would make me look much older than my age.

This behaviour bled over into the rest of my life too. I started dressing more and more maturely at school as well. Girls would shout 'woman' at me as though it was an insult, but secretly I was happy to just be myself, and that meant acting older than I was. I wasn't going to change to please them.

I wanted to look and act the part. But soon I was to take things a little bit too far ...

CHAPTER 4
My First Love

I was fifteen when I took a shine to him. He was a guy that I often saw in the club, and unsurprisingly he was older than me. He was a very good-looking guy, tall and slim with lovely auburn hair and piercing blue eyes. My friend fancied his mate and so we attempted to organise a night out together. We had only arranged to go to the local fair, but I was hoping he'd become my first boyfriend. I was desperate for a taste of that kind of life. That would be taking maturity to a whole new level!

It was a bit comical though when, on the way home from the fair, we passed my old school and I told him that I'd recently been a pupil there. I quickly realised my mistake, and I was rumbled. It's probably just as well that this happened, as it's terrible to lead someone to believe you are older than you really are. To give the lad credit, he did decide that it wouldn't be appropriate to meet again due to the age difference – he was 21, a whole six years older than me.

I was distraught at this. And I was even more miserable when my parents found out. They were livid and banned me from ever seeing him again. And so I found a solution: we carried on seeing each other, platonically, until I reached 16. We were really quite sensible with it all ...

Until we decided, on a whim, to get engaged. Looking back now, I can see it was absolutely crazy, but at the time, I had only one thought: *yes*. I was so determined that this would be my first and only boyfriend, the person that I would marry, and that nothing was going to come between us. How ironic that I was so naive and yet I thought I was being incredibly mature, having waited so long before we could have any kind of romantic relationship. What I will say is that there *was* an enormous level of respect between us, and my boyfriend did eventually manage to win my parents round with the promise of looking after me. His family and friends were obviously shocked when we got together, and I suppose it is understandable, but for the most part they accepted me and I was grateful for that.

It was around this time that I experienced the death of a loved one for the first time. My boyfriend's dad had been suffering with cancer and sadly it claimed his life. It was upsetting for me up to a certain level but the most distressing part was seeing my boyfriend go through such heart-wrenching grief. It was so very heartbreaking. I felt quite helpless but wanted to be around to help him as much as I could. I guess it was a lot for such a young girl to deal with, but I felt an obligation to shoulder some of his pain.

Things weren't to get any easier. I was seventeen now and about to leave school. In all honesty, I'd been feeling as though I'd outgrown school for a while now; further education felt pointless and the other girls didn't seem to be on my wavelength any more. By the time I came to leave, I was just glad to get out of the place. I thought I wanted to go to college but I only lasted a week there. Dad was so annoyed when I left college and demanded to know what I was planning on doing with the rest of my life.

'I dunno,' I shrugged, enraging my dad even further. 'I'm just going to find a job. It'll be fine.'

Somehow, I managed to get lucky and fall on my feet. Susan's dad managed to have a word with his solicitor who offered me a couple of weeks' work experience, and I jumped at the chance. I was really happy in that office, and was in awe watching how quickly and efficiently one of the older girls was in her work. I really admired her;

she was very attractive and smart, and was always so happy and bubbly. I craved her confidence and wished I could be like her. I'd been doing this more and more recently – losing confidence in myself and coveting other people's lives.

After being in the office for only one week, it was time for me to move on as my friend Lesley from school had told me there were still vacancies on a YTS course at ICI Wilton. She'd given me a number to ring to organise an interview and, thankfully, I had been accepted. I left the office with a glowing reference and they assured me that if a vacancy became available they would offer me a job.

I began my YTS scheme and was placed in the printing section where my role was to learn how to operate the machinery along with dealing with the public. I felt so shy in my first couple of weeks at work and I longed to be as sophisticated and able as the other young girls there. I could feel my self-esteem shrivelling up, and it didn't help that I was starting to feel unwell. I started to suffer from horrendous headaches that stopped me from working effectively. As well as this, I was concerned that I wasn't really widening my skill set. Once I had become familiar with the machinery, there was very little else for me to learn.

My dentist had discovered that I had wisdom teeth stuck in the back of my gums and they weren't able to come through as there was not enough room in my mouth. There was also another tooth that had laid itself horizontally across my gum. These two things were causing me absolute agony and I could barely concentrate.

The agony became so unbearable that I had to take time off work, and on the 19th December I went into hospital for an operation which would involve an overnight stay. I also decided that I wanted to start a new placement with the local council after Christmas, because I just felt like I was completely stuck in a rut in my current job. Nothing seemed to be sticking with me and though the girls I worked with were a lovely bunch, I really felt I had to keep moving. I wanted to find meaning in what I was doing and I still hadn't managed to do that.

I felt a little nervous when I went into the hospital, and I felt particularly emotional when I had to sign a consent form. I know it was only an operation for wisdom teeth, but it kind of confirmed for me the possibility that something could go wrong. Maybe it was fear that made me feel vulnerable, or maybe it was something more, but when my boyfriend came in and gave me a lovely 'Get Well' card, I had to stop myself from crying. You see, the card wasn't from him – it was from his friend.

I shouldn't have been shocked, because he'd never been really affectionate. But it hit me hard. I was seriously upset and it took a lot of self-control to put on a brave face. Somehow I managed to, and after saying goodbye to my visitors, I made friends with a couple of other patients. Together we chatted the night away until very late, when we were advised to get some sleep as we had a difficult day ahead of us. I was thankful for the distraction as I felt really quite affected by the card situation. Why had it upset me so badly?

The following morning, I asked the doctor if he would save my teeth for me.

'Yes, that's not a problem,' he responded. I could tell he thought it was strange, but he was discreet about it, which I appreciated. I just wanted to see what had been causing me all the pain!

The next thing I remember is waking up in recovery with my mouth stuffed with cotton wool and lots of bleeding. It felt awful, truly shocking. At some point, I attempted to go to the toilet and when I stood up I was pleased to see that, as I'd been nil-by-mouth the previous day, my tummy felt really flat. I felt great! My bubble was soon burst, though, when another lady pointed out that I might want to look in the mirror.

I was horrified at the image that stared back at me. My face had ballooned. I looked just like a huge hamster and my skin was all black and blue. Panicked, I asked a nurse how long it would take to go back to normal.

'Well, actually, it'll probably start to look worse over the next few days,' the nurse admitted sheepishly. I stared at her in astonishment. Worse? 'There'll be some more swelling and bruising, but it'll calm down after a few days.'

And yet I didn't feel reassured. Anxiety came over me in waves. An irrational part of my mind started tormenting me. What if this wasn't normal after all? What if my face never went back to how it was before? Would I always look like this? Despite the nurse and doctor constantly reminding me that I had gone through an awful lot of trauma to have these teeth removed, I couldn't shake off the fear.

Later that evening I returned home and felt really sorry for myself. But other than a bit of comfort from Mam, I wasn't shown much in the way of sympathy. Dad, his usual unsympathetic self, just couldn't understand why, on attempting to eat a mashed-up tea, I burst into tears. But I couldn't help it! I was in deep pain and I felt traumatised by my experience, as I'd gone through a lot of distress in such a short amount of time. Dad was always of the opinion that it was his way or no way and that it was only his option that mattered. As result, he thought I should just suck it up. He never really showed much understanding for other people's pain. It made him seem very hard at times.

Thankfully, Mam stood up for me as she always did, but it did little to make me feel better. I stared at the little test-tube bottle with my wretched teeth inside it. What a size they were. *Well*, I thought to myself. *Let's just hope it has all been worthwhile.*

A few days later, my boyfriend was going out for an evening at the opening of a room at the local bar. Although I was still very sore and swollen, I wanted to go and join him. I wanted to be out and not stay at home feeling sorry for myself. And so I decided that I would make every effort to get ready, put on some make-up, and join him. Perhaps a night out was exactly what I needed to make me feel better.

But later that evening I began to wish I had stayed at home. This was clearly a mistake. My boyfriend was dressed up in fancy dress and clearly enjoying lots of attention while supposedly fundraising for some pub charity that I really can't recall. I grew increasingly suspicious as a woman started making quite a fuss of him whenever they were in a different room and when they thought I couldn't see them. I might as well have been invisible there for the amount of attention he was paying me. It made me feel worthless. I looked myself up and down, wondering what I'd done wrong. Why wasn't my boyfriend interested in me?

It was a question I'd been asking myself a lot of late. Increasingly I felt neglected. Deep down I knew he wasn't looking after me properly, not in the way that a boyfriend should. I was always doing the chasing. He hadn't made a fuss of me in hospital; I hadn't received any cards or flowers. I had, admittedly, secretly hoped that he'd cancel this night as he knew I was still unwell. I craved his love and some kind of demonstration that he cared. I knew he was taking me for granted, but he was my first love. He was so important to me. At that stage I knew that no matter how bad he made me feel, I didn't want to lose him.

I threw myself into work to distract myself. I started my new work placement at Cargo Fleet Offices after Christmas. I worked very hard in those first few months, and I was rewarded for it – a permanent post came up and all of the staff wanted me to go for it. They had been really impressed with my work and it made me swell with pride. Here, finally, was some validation. It didn't quite make up for my boyfriend's neglect, but I was so fragile that any kind of positivity propped me up.

I was only there for a three-month placement and afterwards I returned to ICI Wilton, waiting for the permanent job to be advertised. I was incredibly bored in ICI headquarters. I delivered post to the various departments and it was soul-destroying. It comes as no surprise then that as soon as the job for the council was advertised,

I applied straight away. I really gave it my all in the interview, and I was delighted when I was offered the job. Here was proof that I was worth something.

My parents were just overjoyed as it was a very big thing back then for someone to secure a job with the local authority. Having my dad's approval was particularly nice. That didn't happen often any more.

I felt so happy and so proud of myself. Now was a chance to really make a difference in the real world, to prove that I was a proper adult at last. Here was the opportunity to prove my worth to someone. It was time to bury all my anxiety, fear, worry, and trauma and throw myself into the world of work. I couldn't wait to start. Perhaps my real life could now really begin!

CHAPTER 5

End of a Dream

I was given a start date for my new job: 22nd April. I was only 17, and so excited.

I suppose the prospect of starting a new job was a way for me to distract myself from niggling worries about my boyfriend. Things were certainly far from happy in my personal life. I'd known for a while that things weren't going well, but what was to come was worse than I could ever imagine.

Ever since my boyfriend had lost his dad, strange things had been happening at his home. He was forever being accused of things going missing. On a number of occasions his mother had left her purse lying around, only to find later that money had been taken from it. There was also money going missing from a local club that he was involved in. I had no evidence that he was really responsible for any of this, but I knew the fallout was going to be bad.

Sure enough, I wasn't wrong.

One evening I went to stay at my boyfriend's house. We had been out for the evening and on returning we just did the usual thing and made ourselves something to eat. His mum was out for the night, staying at her daughter's house for company, and my boyfriend went out to walk the dog.

Feeling full and sleepy, I decided to go to bed. I was really tired. I locked the door, removed the key, and watched out of the window as my boyfriend left with the dog. I went to bed and was asleep within minutes.

The next thing I knew, there was a horrendously loud banging on the door. I woke up instantly and it gave me such a fright. At first, I thought I must have dreamt it as the banging had stopped as soon as it had started. But then there it came again, louder and louder. My heart thudding in my chest, I put on my dressing gown and rushed down the stairs. As I fumbled to get the key in the door, I could hear the shouting voices of numerous men on the other side of the door.

'It's the police. Open up!'

I felt sick to the core as I tried my best to open the door as quickly as I could. Awful thoughts started running through my mind. When I finally managed to open the door, I was amazed to see about five policemen standing in front of me and two police vans near the front gate. I couldn't understand what on earth was happening. I was still dazed from being woken from a deep sleep.

A policeman held up a coat in front of me and asked if it belonged to my boyfriend.

'Yes, it looks like it,' I replied, squinting, blurry-eyed, at the coat. 'But I don't understand ...'

Just then I heard a voice shouting 'Karen, don't tell them anything!' It was my boyfriend's voice. He was inside the van.

But I didn't *know* anything. I was so confused. One of the police officers handed me the dog and informed me that my boyfriend had been arrested for burglary. I barely had any time to process it before they drove off and left me standing there, amazed. Feeling physically sick, I hurried upstairs to get dressed. I was sure that there must have been some mistake; surely my boyfriend would never do anything like that?

I locked the house up and ran over to his sister's house. Luckily they never went to bed early and she and her mother were still awake. I was shaking and stumbling over my words in shock, struggling to tell them what had happened fast enough. I felt validated in my convictions when they looked just as stunned as I felt. Perhaps it was a mistake after all?

Feeling helpless, we just sat there for the rest of the night, drinking tea, trying to make some sense of what had just happened. None of us really slept that night.

Mam wasted no time in telling me to walk away from him the next day. This felt a bit rich, coming from a woman who had never listened to this kind of advice when it came to her own troublesome other half. But there was no doubt in her mind that if he was being accused of it, then he had done it. I guess deep down I too struggled to comprehend how the police could be wrong, but there was still a little stubborn part of me that hated to think badly of people. I at least owed it to my boyfriend to hear his explanation.

His explanation was … interesting. His version of events was as follows:

He was walking past a local supermarket with the dog when he realised the alarm was ringing. He could see that the window had been smashed and, on a whim, had decided to chance his luck and run in and grab some cigarettes. When the police appeared, he threw them over a wall nearby and ran. But the police were too fast for him and he got caught. He was adamant that he hadn't carried out the break-in, but admitted that he'd mistakenly abused an opportunity.

As feeble as this story was, I so wanted to believe him. And so I did. Turns out it was easy to make myself believe what I wanted to, and it wouldn't be the first time. I wasn't willing to accept that any boyfriend of mine would have intentionally planned this and actually gone ahead with it. I even allowed him to convince me he had worn two coats and gloves that night because it was so cold, despite the fact that I hadn't seen him do so.

I was also later told by his family that he had asked them what cigarettes they preferred. They'd had no idea what he was planning at this point. And yet even with this obviously damning piece of information, I just couldn't bear the idea that he'd done this. And so I rejected it. My mind was a powerful tool in times of desperation. I'd been through so much crap over the years that some part of my psyche found it easier to deny any more of it instead of dealing with it.

I even went to court and supported him there. Needless to say, he was found guilty. And yet he never admitted it to me. I think he knew it would disgust me, so he never did. And so this gave me the excuse to carry on with my denial. I blocked any doubt from my mind, and offered to help him raise the money for the fine. I successfully made myself blind to the truth of what was going on.

Mam asked me continuously why I couldn't walk away. She told me that one day I would meet someone who was worthy of my love, and that if I was staying by his side just because we were engaged, then I needed to rethink.

I don't know if that was my reason. Perhaps it was. I had always thought I would marry the first man that I slept with (especially as I tried so hard to be a good Catholic girl) and so maybe that was the reason for my staying power. Walking away from my boyfriend would be to admit defeat, and to accept that another part of my life had failed yet again. I wasn't succeeding at being an adult. And if I wasn't succeeding, what value did I have as a person? The thought terrified me.

Of course, looking back I wish I'd done things differently, because I was about to cause myself a whole load of heartache, illness, and mental distress. My stubbornness and determination to stay with my boyfriend eventually made me very ill.

I suppose the alarm bells should have started ringing when my boyfriend asked me to help him get a personal loan. He asked me to ask Mam if she could get in contact with a chap she knew who did who did personal loans. Mam refused and warned me to stop this before it went too far, but I utterly refused to face the danger head on.

While on a conscious level I tried to smooth over the cracks in what was obviously a failing relationship, clearly my subconscious was having issues. I started to lose sleep.

Whenever I tried to switch off my mind and relax, thoughts and worries raced around my head. One night of lost sleep spiralled into more and soon I was suffering from insomnia. It was a miserable existence. Dad came in from work one morning after a night shift and I asked why I couldn't sleep. He didn't really have a clue about what had been going on; Mam had been smart enough not to tell him. It wasn't worth rousing his temper.

Totally oblivious to what was happening, when I told him I didn't know why I couldn't sleep he just said, 'You must have something on your conscience.'

I honestly think my dad's words jolted me into some kind of action. Something was on my conscience, and while I was blocking out any thoughts that I didn't like during the day, clearly they were coming back to haunt me at night. I clearly wasn't happy with my boyfriend any more and I finally realised I had to end this destructive relationship.

Feeling anxious and a bit sick, I went around to my boyfriend's house to see him. As usual, it turned out he wasn't there, but in the pub instead. I decided to wait for him to come back, but it was hours and I grew impatient and fed up. I guessed I'd have to do it another day.

As I headed off towards the bus stop, I bumped into him. Taking a deep breath to steady my nerves, I stopped him in his tracks. 'It's over,' I said. 'I love you, but I don't love your money problems and your other issues.'

I stared at him, willing him to show some kind of emotion. But none came. He didn't seem to care. He looked down at me with cold, empty eyes as I sobbed. He barely even flinched when I ran off and caught the bus home. I was distraught. It was yet another indication of how little value I had in someone else's eyes.

What was going on with my life?

CHAPTER 6

Spiralling

The sleepless nights continued. I carried on going into work, but I was unable to concentrate and I couldn't function. I also felt really uncomfortable there. There was a situation unfolding and every time one of the girls left the office the other women would start bitching about her.

This really didn't sit well with me as, despite everything I'd been through, I still believed in the inherent good nature of people and I was finding all the negativity to be too much. This girl was lovely and was doing her best to train me. And if this was how they behaved towards her, maybe they were also doing it to me? Maybe everyone hated me as well?

The lack of sleep, heartache, low self-esteem, and the constant worry was starting to affect my appetite. I could barely eat and found myself struggling to cope with everyday life. It felt like my mind was starting to crack. Whenever I walked outside I felt like a tiny, insignificant person in a massive world. I no longer had any idea what I was doing; I started to throw equipment away at work instead of filing invoices. I was a complete and total mess. I could feel that I was heading for a breakdown and my mind convinced me that there was no one to catch me.

But there was. My manager sensed how unwell I was becoming. I was caught in a downward spiral. One day while I was at work, she went to visit Mam to explain that I was very poorly and I must be kept at home.

I was running around like a wild animal, completely oblivious to reality. I just needed someone to stop me and take a hold of me and steer me in the right direction. When Mam realised how serious things were, she made an appointment to see the GP.

It was an incredibly stressful time for both my mam and for me. Things really began to escalate. I was irritable, swearing in anger at people in the surgery. My mam was mortified but kept it together as I was prescribed anti-depressants.

I'm not sure what I expected of the doctor. Maybe I just wanted him to wave a magic wand and make everything go away. But to be honest, even though I remember most of what happened now, I know that at the time I didn't have any control over anything. My imagination was just running riot and I was half in and half out of reality. I was quickly becoming more and more deluded, but I was so out of it that I couldn't really articulate it.

One day, to try to make my mind off things, Mam took me to the prize bingo night. Some days I was okay, and sometimes I really wasn't, but it wasn't easy for Mam to tell. This night she hadn't spotted the signs of my agitation. I wanted to leave, but she kept insisting that I wait for her while she played the 'Free go', whatever that meant. I pushed and pushed her to come with me, but she wasn't having any of it.

For reasons I still cannot fathom to this day, I reacted to this by running out of the bingo hall and into the club that I used to visit quite often. I think I had an idea in my head that I was going to a surprise party. There was no rational thought process behind this; it was another one of my delusional episodes. I ran into the club and attempted to open the door to the upstairs room, which of course was locked as it was the middle of the day. The doorman shouted at me to come downstairs, telling me that I couldn't go in there. But I didn't listen. It took him and my mam, who'd followed me from the bingo hall, to pull me away before I would stop. I personally had no idea what on earth was happening. I was so ill; I couldn't stop myself. Mam was terrified; she'd never seen anyone have a mental breakdown before.

The weeks following this were incredibly hard for everyone involved. But slowly but surely, my medication started to kick in, and I started getting some sleep. This was vital. In fact, it made me feel so much better that I momentarily thought that returning to work would be a good idea. I'd only been there a few weeks and I didn't want to be seen as a failure in a brand-new job. My Dad was also piling on the pressure, telling me at every opportunity that I would be sacked. The problem was that he just didn't understand that I was mentally ill. The more he rushed me back to work, the more trouble it was causing as I was just not well enough to function. The added stress and pressure was hurting me rather than helping me. Nevertheless, I returned, much to my own detriment.

Reality hit home when I received a written warning from work. It stated that my attitude was not appropriate and my standard of work was non-existent. Mam contacted my overall manager, the housing officer, and explained the situation. The manager was very nice to her and took it well, explaining that I wouldn't lose my job. But she stressed the importance of my being looked after properly. I can imagine it wasn't an easy thing for Mam to hear, who was trying her best to help me get well.

There were so many bizarre things happening in my mind at this point. One evening we were watching *Crimewatch* on the TV and I became convinced that my ex-boyfriend had committed the crimes. I was started to whisper as I thought that the house was bugged and that I was being recorded. Dad was very concerned at this point, and it opened his eyes to the seriousness of my condition. I told him, very seriously, that there were people in the garden listening to what I was saying.

'There's no one out there,' he tried to reassure me, clearly terrified of my behaviour. 'No one is listening to you except me.' But of course this didn't get through to me. I was too far gone.

As the weeks continued, I mentioned on many occasions that I was confused. It became my most used word. I just felt a constant state of confusion, and nothing I did or said seemed to help.

I felt lost and alone and I was still suffering from the heartache of my lost relationship. I felt isolated and cut off from my friends. I hadn't been in touch with my old school friends for a long time and my work colleagues didn't want to associate with me outside of work. Mam had Dad, my sister had her husband and children, but I was completely on my own. It made me feel like a young child again, and that was not a place I wanted to return to. Not now when everyone else had moved on. What an epic way to fail at everything I'd felt was important in life.

I continued to take my tablets, though they didn't do a lot to help. I was then allocated my first ever psychiatrist, but we only met for a single meeting before he handed me back to my GP. He gave up on me immediately, and I had no idea why.

I was pretty devastated to see the psychiatrist's name on my appointment card. I suppose I felt a little uncomfortable as many people back then only thought that those doctors were allocated to patients who had 'lost the plot' or 'gone round the bend'. These were very sad descriptions for those who were simply suffering from mental health issues and they were particularly terrifying for me. Stigma was rife back then and there was no real level of understanding.

The psychiatrist was a bizarre sort of man. He just asked lots of questions and did an awful lot of mumbling. It was a very strange feeling, as it was the first time I had talked to a stranger in such an open way, to be sitting there answering lots of questions about my personal life, my complex family, and my relationships. I felt comfortable enough to open up to him, but I didn't get the sense that he understood me at all. He identified some of my thinking problems but advised me to tackle them in a very logical way, and this felt almost impossible for someone as mentally ill as myself.

He told me, quite earnestly, that I didn't have a problem with any amount of work as I was intelligent enough to be able to handle it. He said he felt my problem lay with people. He explained that I was overly concerned with what people thought about me and that, going forward, I should wear imaginary blinkers and not allow people to bother me. He was incredibly accurate with that description, but unfortunately, I never really put his advice into action. It was one thing telling me what I needed to do, but quite another to equip me with the tools to do it. I just wasn't well enough. Logic would only get me so far.

When I returned to the GP, the only diagnosis I received was 'anxiety and depression'. It meant nothing to me. I know now that this was because not only was there a real lack of communication between me and the doctor, but it was actually a false diagnosis. As a result, no one really knew what to do with me, let alone myself.

What really added to my stress is that my ex continuously tried to reconcile things with me. He tried all sorts of things to get to me, including contacting my nana Lizzie. But despite my loneliness, I wasn't having any of it. Getting through every single day was hard, and I couldn't handle his baggage as well as mine. I needed some kind of positivity.

The next few months were particularly hard, and my behaviour became worse and more erratic. I did struggle with anxiety and depression, but it was just part of a bigger, wider, more ominous issue for me. I stayed at home all day every day, eating and eating to fill some kind of empty void inside of me. My confidence and self-esteem plummeted and a blanket of sadness settled over my shoulders.

My parents were at a complete loss; even my dad started to feel some kind of sympathy for me. In his desperation, he bought me a pet poodle named Pepi, who I loved dearly. But of course it was no substitution for medication or therapy. He brightened up my life a bit but still I struggled on, wading through the quagmire of my own mind with no idea of how to pull myself out of it.

CHAPTER 7

Going Back to Go Forward

As the months passed my mood continued to fluctuate. I decided to stop my medication as it didn't seem to be helping me. As it turned out, that was okay. Slowly but surely I felt myself getting a little bit stronger. But I still craved love and attention and company, and so I made a really unwise decision. I decided to call my ex-boyfriend and arrange to meet up.

I knew that this was a bit of a U-turn. But it was Christmas, that time of year that makes many of us feel the need for companionship. By this point I was feeling a bit mentally stronger and certainly not prepared to put up with any nonsense.

It would have been my parents' idea of a nightmare, had I told them my plans. It was last thing they wanted for me. I'm sure if I'd told them at the time, they would have feared for my wellbeing again. And who could have blamed them?

But of course I wasn't thinking rationally. I just needed to feel that I belonged to someone again, that I had some value again. He was the only person at that time who I felt I could turn to. I needed to move on from 1986 as it had been a very cruel year. Perhaps this was not the best way forward, but I needed to try before I completely gave up on life. I was completely desperate.

It was Christmas Eve when I called him. I had been out with the family and didn't want to be on my own any longer. He seemed surprised to hear from me, but we arranged to meet the following day and go for a drink together. I wasn't fully well and looking back, I know it wasn't a wise thing to do. But hindsight, especially when well, is a wonderful thing.

We did a lot of talking and decided to try and start over again.

To begin with, it was a secret – we had little sneaky meetings until we felt that there was no point in hiding it any more. Eventually we told people that we were trying to make a go of it again. Needless to say, people didn't think it was the best idea I'd ever had. Lots of people told me that it was a mistake. But honestly, I really didn't care. In my ongoing delusions, I honestly felt that he was the only person who'd been there for me throughout all the bad stuff that happened to me. I didn't feel like I could trust anyone else; they'd all sat back and watched the breakdown happen. To be honest, I hadn't felt that anyone had really given me any support. How I hadn't ended up in hospital is beyond me. I had been so poorly.

Things were a bit of a challenge at work. At first people had found it very hard to forget about my breakdown. I don't think they understood what it had all been about and for some time they held it against me. The girls were very reserved towards me and at times they were quite hostile.

But I was determined to keep my job. I worked extra hard so that I was soon back up to the standard I was working at prior to my illness. I was just muddling through it, trying to keep my head above water, taking tentative steps to throw myself back into normal life. My relationship wasn't brilliant, but at first, I convinced myself that it had to be better than nothing.

Gradually, though, I was changing. Unlike when we argued last time, I was stronger, more resilient, and found it easier to just walk away. I no longer sat in his house during the evenings, waiting for him to grace me with his presence. Instead I would go to the local with my family while he met the lads at the club on a Friday night. I felt more independent.

As I started to socialise a bit more and get back in touch with old friends, a realisation dawned on me. There was a good life to be had without my boyfriend. I can't say that things weren't better than the first time around, but they were far from perfect. And we both seemed to want different things. This became so apparent when, to everyone's amazement, my sister Susan discovered she was pregnant again. Her son, Shaun, was born in the February. I was in awe of the beautiful child and this just confirmed for me what I always knew deep down: I wanted to be a mother more than anything. It was also clear that my boyfriend was in no rush for this to happen and it made me question our future.

I was also starting to develop a strong work ethic again. I knew that to get to where I wanted to be in life I needed to be in a good job, but he thought differently. He had been in work before but he was unemployed now, and he'd lost all interest in looking for further work. To me, that made us incompatible. The writing was on the wall: this was never going to work out. It was just a matter of how long it would last. I kept things going for a short while, although I'm not entirely sure why I bothered. As my confidence grew, I knew it was time for change.

That time came in September. I happened to be at a barbeque in my local club and found myself enjoying the company of another man. A much older man. He was also married.

I enjoyed the flirting and it made me all too aware of the fact that the time had come to end things with my boyfriend. I had just simply had enough and here I could see prospects of something altogether more exciting.

That night we had a massive argument at his house. I took that as my opportunity to get up and walk away. I knew it was truly all over now. This time he tried to fight harder for me, but there was no going back on my decision.

What followed was, I admit now, a pattern of behaviour caused by my own naivety. I loved it when people showed an interest in me. Knowing what I know now – that my mental health played a huge part in how I behaved during this point in my life – I never would have done what I did. Although I'd always felt very mature, I obviously had a lot to learn. And the notion of not taking up with married men was clearly one of them.

But, nevertheless, I moved full steam ahead. I think part of it came from knowing that these relationships were never going to be anything more than shallow. After falling in so deep with the first, I don't think I wanted that again. I used this move as an escape from being held down by one person. I was enjoying the attention, and wanted nothing more. Being constantly told that I looked lovely was a novelty for me. I thrived on being taken out to places that I hadn't visited before. I was never truly in it for the money, although that is probably what some would think. I rarely accepted huge gifts from these men, and always paid my own way as much as I could. It was the experience I loved. It was exhilarating.

It was at this point in my life that I experienced my first real taste of stigma against mental illness. One of my colleagues was retiring and I had always been told the job would be mine. Imagine, then, my shock and disappointment when the job was given to another girl.

'But why?' I asked my manager, fuming inside but keeping as calm as possible. They told me that the reason I didn't get it was because of my mental breakdown. I would have to prove myself all over again, and show them that my illness wouldn't affect my work.

But that wasn't all.

'Karen, we need you to help the new girl settle in and get her up to scratch with the various systems.'

Charming, I thought, feeling very annoyed. But I kept quiet. Through gritted teeth I helped the new girl settle in and helped her wherever I could. After all, it wasn't her fault that she got the job over me. I buried the resentment deep inside myself and we managed to become good friends. I never quite shook off that feeling of resentment, though.

No matter, I thought. Life was fun anyway. A few people looked down at me because they didn't approve of my personal life, but I didn't let it get to me. At the time I didn't really think about my new man's wife. I'd become good at blocking things out of my mind and I did that with her, to make my own life easier. In my mind that was okay because I wasn't the person who was married. I know, I know – it was wrong. But I didn't care at all then.

It was only a matter of time, though, until I decided that I did want more than just to be the other woman. He promised me over and over again that he would leave his wife for me, and like most women in this situation, I believed him. It took me a while before I realised he never would. And that didn't sit well with me. My self-esteem and state of mind depended heavily on feeling like I was something special. Slowly I started to crave more validation again. So what did I do? I got involved with a chap through work.

I am shocked to think, now, that I was capable of seeing two men at the same time with no guilty conscience. But that is what happened, and I can't change the past. Maybe part of me felt that they were also cheating on me in a way; that way I could justify it to myself. That way, I wasn't the bad one.

1989 came fast and sudden. I'd been living life on a high and generally I felt really happy. But one night in April things changed in a horrific fashion.

My friend Michele invited me on a night out in Redcar. We were having a brilliant time. We moved on to a nightclub, feeling a bit tipsy and carefree. I guess I wasn't being very careful as I was dancing because I accidentally knocked a woman with my flailing arms. She didn't like this one bit. I apologised to her, but she turned quite nasty.

'What the hell do you think you're doing?' she snarled at me, looking furious. I shrank back, intimidated, but the bouncer came and warned her off. I assumed that was the end of it and carried on dancing.

But later that night, back on the dancefloor, I found myself alone when Michele found a lad to go dancing with. I didn't mind this much as I was swaying to music and minding my own business. At least I was, until suddenly I was pushed to the floor.

In the darkness it took me a few seconds to realise that it was the woman from before who'd knocked me down. She straddled me and started to attack me. It was horrendous. I thought she was attacking me with a knife. With each strike I felt deep cuts being slashed across my face. I screamed loudly but felt powerless to stop her.

Eventually she was dragged off me by bouncers and some of the other dancers. I stumbled to my feet in a state of shock. Still reeling, I struggled to concentrate on what was going on around me. Someone somewhere shouted that I might want to go to the ladies and take a look in the mirror. The pain started to kick in as I made my way to the toilets.

As I looked in the mirror I could barely make out my own face. It was dripping with blood and covered in deep wounds. I cried and screamed and went searching for Michele. She was nowhere to be seen and so I panicked and ran out into the street. I could just make out a taxi nearby with a chap climbing in. He took one look at the state of me and told me to jump in, letting me share his taxi and thankfully ensuring that I got home alright.

Mam and Dad were horrified at the sight of me when I burst into their bedroom. My memory is hazy after that. All I really remember is that they took me straight to the hospital where nurses stitched up my face. I remember feeling sick – traumatised and defiled.

The following morning Mam got straight on the phone to the nightclub. She demanded information and reported the incident to the police, who then came around to take statements, promising that the woman would be caught. They had a name and there had been witnesses, so it didn't take them long to catch her. Michele came over that day. She was absolutely mortified when Dad opened the door and shouted in her face, asking her where on Earth she had got to and why she hadn't been around to protect me. She burst into tears, apologising over and over again.

'I'm your friend,' she said to me, hugging me and sobbing. 'I should have been there to protect you.'

I shook my head, to the best of my ability when my face was full of stitches. 'I don't blame you,' I said. 'You didn't do anything wrong.'

'I thought you'd maybe met someone like I did and was off dancing with them,' she said. 'But I should have been around to help you.'

I shook my head. I told her that I wasn't going to stop being her friend over it all. It wasn't her fault that this had happened to me.

Over the next few days I did what I was best at: tamped down my feelings and tried to carry on like nothing was happening. I went straight back to work, unwilling to admit to anyone what had happened. No one quite knew what to say to me. A rumour started that I'd been in a car accident. I didn't argue against this; it did look that way. They all told me how brave I was and I thrived on it. I wasn't prepared to hide away because of this. I wasn't willing to be a victim. I'd done that once before at the hands of my mental illness, and there was no way I was going back to that dark, awful place.

For this reason I had every intention of going on my planned trip to Blackpool that weekend, wearing sunglasses to hide my now black eyes. I convinced myself that this was just what I needed as it made me get straight back out onto the social scene, back into the nightclubs again. It was my way of showing defiance. Michele helped me iron and pack, bless her. Then off I went with my friend Carol, laughing when one of the lads named me 'Miss Zacks', the name of the nightclub. I was still able to make myself laugh about it. I still had my humour intact!

The truth, however, has a tendency to out itself and soon people at work found out about what had really happened. One lovely girl, Janice, informed me that her dad had worked for the police and would try his hardest to locate the girl in question. I wasn't disappointed: three weeks later, she was arrested.

It was only a matter of time before the reality of what had happened on that evening really hit me. I suppose I had been too busy thinking about my few days away to take in the events of that night. To think it was all because I had knocked the girl accidentally. If that was all it took in life for bad things to happen, how was I to cope the next time I accidentally messed up? Fear hung over me like a dark cloud and I suddenly felt anxious and nervous on a daily basis.

The woman involved appeared in court and had insisted on pleading not guilty. However, when her solicitor had produced the photographs of me in such a state and her with not a mark on her, she was advised it would not be in her best interests to do this. I was so relieved to be told that she had decided to plead guilty and face the consequences. I knew I couldn't face having to go to court and go through the horrific ordeal all over again. I certainly never wanted to see her face again. When asked why she had assaulted me like that, she'd said, 'I thought I would get the first one in.' After hearing that, I knew that she was just pure evil. My faith in humanity was diminished.

On the day of the court hearing she was given a fourteen-day prison sentence and ordered to pay me a ridiculous amount of £75. What an absolute joke! I felt that what she had done to me deserved at least a longer prison sentence; she could have killed me that night. The amount of money seemed so pathetic, like that was how little I was worth. Yet another body blow to my already teetering self-esteem.

I still wonder if she learnt anything from that, if she ever changed. It had a detrimental effect on me and I found it so hard to move on from it. I felt nervous all the time, especially if I was ever in a public place and an altercation was taking place. She had scarred me mentally as well as physically, but I had to try my hardest to put this behind me and move on with my life. The facial scars never really disappeared but just faded over time. A constant reminder of my trauma and my perceived worth.

My apparent lack of worth was only reinforced when I realised that my continuing affair with my married older man was never going to go anywhere. I know now that it was for the best, considering the situation and the age gap. Towards the end of August, we had a row and I stormed off. I later learnt through one of his friends that he'd gone off on holiday with his wife. That was the confirmation I needed to know that I was nothing to him. Our fall out didn't bother him in the least. He had no intention of leaving his wife. He was yet another person who didn't care about me at all.

At this stage I could feel myself becoming more self-aware. I felt like garbage; I'd been damaged, hurt and abused. I'd been shown how little I meant to both certain individuals and the system as a whole. And I was sick of it.

I knew I deserved more. I deserved to be happy, and I deserved to be loved.

CHAPTER 8
Something Better Lies Ahead

I should probably say that I wholly believe in fate. And it's a good job really, as it was about to work its magic on my life.

One night I decided to have an evening out with Mam and Dad. We went off to a pub not that far away from where we lived. Mam and I sat in the lounge and Dad went into the bar to be with his mates, but after an hour or so we thought it'd be a good idea to join Dad and the lads in the bar. We always managed to have a good laugh with them.

As we sat there, talking away, I happened to notice a really good-looking lad who was working behind the bar. He had a gorgeous smile and beautiful eyes. Of course, I made the mistake of telling Dad's mate, who couldn't resist telling him when he went to order a pint! I blushed and turned away, acting innocent and oblivious. I wasn't confident enough to approach him!

I didn't think any more of this until we were stood waiting for the bus at the end of the night. A mixture of excitement and nerves swirled around in my tummy as I saw the lad from behind the bar walking towards us. My face went bright red as he introduced himself as Peter. I smiled and tried to act as sophisticated as possible – a bit difficult when I felt hot and flustered.

To my delight he got onto the bus with me and sat next to me. We enjoyed a good chat on our way home, and then and there he asked me on a date. A few nights later we were having drinks together in Redcar. It all happened incredibly quickly.

He won me over straight away. He had a wicked sense of humour and he really made me laugh. Conversation came easy and the night was a lot of fun without us having to try too hard or put in a lot of effort to impress each other. I loved it. Something about this felt different to how it was with my first boyfriend. Peter felt special to me straight away. I could already sense that this was going to go well.

In my professional life, an opportunity to apply for the job I really wanted came up again. The new girl in the office announced that she was expecting a baby and I was asked to cover her job while she went on maternity leave. After a few months, she decided not to return, and again I was told that I'd be seriously considered for it.

But I thought about this carefully. I'd been in this situation before and had felt really disappointed when it didn't come to fruition. For that reason, I decided to apply for a post with Middlesbrough Borough Council instead. I was invited for an interview and got the job. I was absolutely overjoyed, as I'd been applying non-stop for other jobs as well. I'd had numerous interviews in Langbaurgh, all to no avail. I was getting to the point where I thought I'd never achieve anything big or prove myself. That anxious, unhappy Karen was starting creep back – the one who felt worthless if she wasn't constantly moving forward. And that was a shame, because I'd been feeling really confident.

It was also a great opportunity to leave my dodgy past behind. I wouldn't have to see the guy I'd been sleeping with any more. I could start somewhere new and have a fresh start, where people didn't know about my mental health issues.

Nevertheless, I still felt incredibly sad when the time came for me to leave my job. I was about to make a huge change in my life and God knows I hadn't handled those well in the past. My last day was on my 21st birthday and I felt a weird mix of elation and panic. I dulled the nerves with drink when my workmates took me out to the local pub for a farewell lunch. Drinking during working hours was less frowned upon then, as long as you didn't get too carried away.

I suppose it was this day that made me realise how much my self-esteem depended on how others thought of me. Lots of people came to the pub to send me off, and Peter was there serving behind the bar. I felt popular and wanted. I felt celebrated and I knew I was going to be missed. I loved it. It made me quite emotional. I was really going to miss them all.

When I got home I laid down on my bed and had a little cry. I read through the cards I'd received, wondering if I'd made the right decision and hoping I wouldn't regret it. But I pulled myself together, sobered up, and headed back out with Peter and my family to celebrate my birthday.

How I stayed standing upright that night still amazes me; I'd had a *lot* to drink. I felt happy and carefree. Sometime that night on the dancefloor, Peter asked me to marry him. I think we were both a bit high on life and obviously incredibly drunk. I shouted 'YES' into his ear as we carried on dancing. I had no idea if he was even being serious. It all seems hilarious now. We'd only been seeing each other for a month, but I'd been so through so much crap in the past that I saw no issues with grasping life by the horns and going with it. Time would tell if he was 'The One' anyway.

My mood continued to be governed by other people's opinions. Despite how much growing up I'd done, despite having been through a horrific mental breakdown, that still hadn't really changed.

The new job was nice enough but it was a very different experience working for another local authority. At my last job we had referred to all the managers by their first names; and they had felt like our mates. But here senior management all seemed a bit stiff and formal. It also felt a little awkward at first, because the young lad who was training me had also applied for the job, and it was fairly obvious that his colleagues felt he should have got it. I was sorry he hadn't got it, but I insisted that I had the right experience. I panicked slightly. Did this mean the staff didn't like me? I still wasn't sure I could cope with that.

The job was also boring. Really boring. I was spending all of my day crawling around the floor, checking bundles of files in order to find misplaced ones. How dull could a job be? In my second week of doing this I was becoming so fed up that I threw myself into my seat and let go of a few expletives. I ranted and raved, going on about how I was used to working on the budget and making difficult decisions, not crawling round the floor all day. I didn't see myself as a diva, just someone who was stating the obvious. As I calmed down, though, I realised how I must have come across. I went quiet and eyed my workmates nervously.

Suddenly I heard someone burst out laughing. 'Yes!' shouted a girl next to me, clapping. 'She's one of us!'

Huh?

I must have looked quite bewildered, but she went on to explain. For a short while the girls had thought that my quietness meant that I was 'well to do' and not very fun. I could feel the heat of embarrassment rising up my body, but then she continued.

'It's fine now,' she reassured me. 'At least we know you're good fun and one of us now. It's good to see you let go of a bit of frustration!'

I smiled at her, relieved. Who cared if the job was boring? People liked me! I was worthy!

CHAPTER 9

There's a First for Everything . . . And a Second

It seems to me now, looking back on my story, that tragedy always seemed to follow a period of happiness or good health.

Nana Maisie, my dad's mam, had not been very well for quite some time. But it had been a while since I'd seen her regularly. As kids grow up it's quite common to spend a lot of time with their grandparents, and I certainly did that when I was young. But as I began to find my own way in the world, I became more and more distant from Nana. By the time her illness kicked in, it had been many years since I had actually stayed over at house, but I do recognise now that that's fairly normal. But it was the lack of interest I showed that makes me feel guilty then.

I was aware that Nana was struggling living in her house, but because Uncle Barry was still at home that was where she stayed. A lot of family members said that she'd be better off in a home, but to be honest I never really understood the true extent of what was going on. Besides, care homes weren't as common back then. They were frowned upon much more than they are now.

Mam's friend lived opposite Nana Maisie and told us a few stories about how confused she was becoming. And whenever I did manage to visit her, she would often ask me the same questions over and over again. I heard the word dementia mentioned quite a lot but in my ignorance I assumed that that was something that happened to most of the elderly. I don't think I comprehended at that time just how harrowing a condition it actually is.

Dad often came home from his mam's looking concerned and distressed, but he was powerless to do very much as my uncle refused to let their mother leave the family home. It was only a council house, and so it wasn't a financial decision. He just didn't want to lose her; he was quite a lonely man himself.

Whenever Dad came home and cried it hurt me. I'd had a lot of issues with him in the past and I still couldn't show him a lot of affection, but it exposed to me a whole new side of him. I'd hardly ever seen him cry in my whole life, but this confirmed to me that he was still a human in there deep down, despite all the violence over the years.

It was gut-wrenching. He had always tried to hide his emotions over the years. And now seeing him break down in tears proved to me that he was just an ordinary man who was afraid of losing his mother. He clearly wasn't as 'hard' as he wanted everyone to believe.

'How do you think it feels for me when my own mam doesn't recognise me?' he asked me one night, his head in his hands. I guess now he understood what it was like seeing your mother so vulnerable, although that didn't really enter my mind at the time. We just stayed silent, really. Mam and I didn't really know what to say to make him feel any better. There were no words to do that. All we could do was be as understanding as possible.

It was clear that Nana Maisie had Alzheimer's disease. It was far less common then and wasn't often talked about. As a result I didn't understand the full extent of the diagnosis. Thank God there is more awareness of this horrible disease that tears lives and families apart now.

The confusion carried on for some time, but then poor Nana was taken into hospital. Despite how uncomfortable this must have been for him, Peter came with us to give me moral support. Dad was convinced that she wouldn't be coming home. Apparently, as soon as the name Poole Hospital was mentioned, everyone knew what this meant. Apparently it was known as the hospital where people went to end their lives in peace and dignity.

I've been through some harrowing stuff in my time but that night was one of the most heartbreaking for me. I can vividly remember Nana holding out her hand to clutch mine. She was very aware that we were all there with her, but she was very weak and couldn't say a lot. We could tell that holding our hands was her way of saying goodbye to us. My chest ached and I did my best to stop the tears from falling; I didn't want to scare her. When it was time for us to leave, we all kissed her, knowing deep down that we were saying our last goodbyes. I'll never forget the look in Dad's eyes: that knowledge that he was losing his mother.

The next morning the phone rang. I'd joined Mam in bed with a cup of tea. We didn't answer the phone; we left it for Dad to pick up. We knew what was coming.

'That was the hospital. Our old lady has passed way,' Dad called up the stairs. That was the term Dad always used for his mam, and 'lady' was such an accurate description. We hurried downstairs and tried hard to console Dad as we wept our own tears of grief.

It was incredibly hard to get used to the notion that I'd never see Nana Maisie again. This was my first real bereavement and I struggled to cope. I couldn't wrap my head around the notion that my nana, the woman I had spent so much time with in my youth, was no longer around.

In true Karen style, I found a way to switch off my emotions and block out the pain. I was asked to help out with the funeral plans and I threw myself into the task. I selected the hymns as I knew her favourites. I made the decision that she would be taken to the church as it had played such an important role in her life. She found great comfort in there and it seemed fitting to take her there in death. I got through the funeral by keeping myself busy and only allowing myself to think about positive memories, almost as though I was keeping her alive in my head. It was the only thing that kept the desperate ache and longing out of my head and my heart. I felt that I could feel her presence around me, although I still have no idea if she was truly there or not.

Oddly enough, sometime later my boyfriend was to have what he truly believed was a little visit from Nana. Not a lot of people believe in this kind of thing, but it made us happy. A few months had passed since her death when Peter found that he had to move out of his house. I told Mam about it, as I knew I wanted to make a go of our relationship and marry him one day, so I was considering moving in with him. But Mam didn't want me to leave home, so she discussed with Dad the possibility of us just living with them instead. It did seem to make sense because Dad was working away, so it would mean Mam had some company and we would save some money.

One morning Peter came bursting into the kitchen, itching to tell us what he'd seen the previous night. He told us that the bedroom was completely dark and, as he went to turn in to go to sleep, an old lady's face had come from the corner of the room towards him. He said she was smiling and appeared to be wearing a headscarf. He hadn't panicked, as he was convinced it was Nana. Perhaps she was pleased that he had been there at the end for her. We were sure that it was her sign of approval to us too. Whatever the reason, it made us feel all warm inside and soothed our grief for a short while.

Over those next few months I did my best to process my grief while getting on with life, but it was hard. I felt low for a long time. Grief hung like a weight around my neck. I found myself looking for things to distract myself with, again and again and again. And perhaps it was for this reason that getting engaged to Peter made me feel so much better.

Towards the end of the year Peter arrived at my work and rushed me off at lunchtime to buy an engagement ring. He had seen one he thought I would love and he wasn't wrong. Although we'd planned to wait until the following year to get engaged, when the dust had settled and we had a bit more money, we decided that there was no point in waiting. We'd do it at Christmas instead.

Peter did it the old-fashioned way – by asking Dad's permission. Thank God he approved! We went to a dinner dance at a hotel where once again he asked me to marry him. I accepted, delighted, thrilled to have something positive to look forward to once again. I'd started to see a pattern in my thought processes – as long as I always had something positive to look forward to and distract me from my mental state, I stayed stable.

But life isn't always as simple as that, is it?

One of the most terrible nights of my life came upon us the following May. We received a phone call at around eleven – that shrill, loud phone trilling that cuts through the silence and stops your heart. I jumped out of bed, confused and bewildered as to who would be calling so late.

'Hello?' I said into the phone, bleary-eyed and half-asleep.

'Karen,' said my sister Susan, speaking in a very slow and hushed tone. 'Can you come around to my house and have a brandy with me?'

'What?' I was utterly baffled. Why was she asking me this? It was almost midnight! 'What's going on?'

She began to sob. 'It's John,' she explained, breathing heavily. 'Some of his friends have just told me that John's been in a motorcycle accident. I think he's dead.'

I felt as though I was going to throw my entire insides up. 'No, no. Susan, this will be wrong.'

'I don't think so.'

'I'm on my way,' I yelled into the phone as I rushed to grab my clothes. I woke up Mam and Peter, telling them that something had gone terribly wrong.

There was an awful, eerie feeling at Susan's house. We all sat together quietly, waiting for the police to arrive. I believe Glenn called them, but to be honest the build-up to the visit is very hazy to me now.

It wasn't long before we heard the dreaded knock on the door. As the police officer walked in, he began by telling us what we already knew: that there had been a terrible accident. It was Glenn who was brave enough to ask the question we all wanted to ask.

'Was it fatal?' he asked. When the officer confirmed it was, I almost collapsed. I didn't want to acknowledge what I was hearing. I wanted to pretend it wasn't happening, to block it out of my mind like I always did. I just about managed to hold it together as Susan and Glenn were led to the officer's car and taken to identify the body.

Susan seemed strangely calm. I think she was in deep shock, whereas I couldn't stop my mind from going at a hundred miles per minute. What about Glenn Jr and Shaun, who were tucked up in bed oblivious to what was happening? Maybe the police had made a mistake? And if it wasn't, if it was all real, how could we ever move on from this? How could I take so much grief all at once?

My memory of the rest of that night is still a little blurred. I know we went home and sat and cried, talking over the same points over and over again, wondering what on earth had happened on that road. And then suddenly it hit us all that there was one person who was totally unaware of this tragedy. It was poor Nana Lizzie.

She idolised John. She loved all her grandchildren and great-grandchildren, but we all knew that John was her favourite by far. He was the one she worshipped.

The following morning, we talked to Susan and she too worried how she could tell Nana this terrible news. Mam and Susan did not want her to know; they couldn't bring themselves to face Nana. But I knew there was no way we couldn't tell her. She had a right to be told by her close family and not by a total stranger in a local shop or gossipers in the street. And so it was left to me and Peter to head over to her house and break the horrific news.

As she opened her door, we just looked at her, not saying a word. There was a look of panic in her eyes as she read our faces. In a weird kind of way it was as if she was bracing herself for bad news. I had barely whispered John's name before she let out this awful, high-pitched wailing noise. I told her there's been a tragic accident but I didn't need to say any more. I held her in my arms, but my own heart could barely take what had happened. I didn't know how I was to shoulder her pain as well.

The next couple of weeks passed in a blurry, nightmarish haze. I stayed home from work, unable to face anyone. I couldn't put it into words what losing my 19-year-old nephew, who I'd grown up with and loved as a brother, did to my soul and my mental state. It hurt just to think.

It didn't help that rumours were circulating about the nature of John's death. The official story didn't sit right with me. All we knew for certain was that John was on a motorcycle when he hit a fence that surrounded a scrapyard. But the circumstances around it were a mystery as John's friends all told us conflicting stories – who he was with, why he was where he was, why he'd lost control.

But to be honest, after a while we stopped trying to figure out the truth. It seemed only appropriate, out of respect for his parents, that all the stories came to an end. It was not going to change the outcome. What news could be worse for anyone? How could speculating ever bring back our beloved boy?

One of the hardest parts for me was viewing John's body. When the chapel had contacted my sister to tell her that her son's body was ready to view, she'd insisted on going alone. But her husband Glenn asked me to go with her: he didn't think she could cope on her own. I was happy to help, but the whole experience hurt me. My body wracked with sobs as I looked down at my beautiful nephew lying in a coffin, dressed in a smart white designer tracksuit. I swear I felt my sister's heart break as she looked down at his lifeless body, his hands poised almost as though they were still gripping the motorbike. I will never forget that day for as long as I live.

On the day of his funeral, the traffic was held up with lines of cars heading towards the church. It was really quite surreal to see the sheer number of people who had turned out to pay their last respects to John. It was then, I think, that the reality of my nightmare finally hit me: I was at the funeral of that little boy I had grown up with, the baby I had nursed when he was first born. How could life be so cruel? Why did it have to end this way?

As poor John was lowered into the ground after the ceremony, our poor Nana threw some coins onto the coffin.

'There's your pocket money, son,' she whispered.

I broke down and sobbed.

CHAPTER 10
Here We Go Again

Planning my wedding was the only thing that kept my mind occupied. Having complicated plans to focus on kept my fragile mind intact and kept my head above the water. I was grateful for this. I also threw myself back into work – anything to numb the pain of loss that had bruised my heart so badly.

We had to keep a close eye on Nana Lizzie, who had suffered a couple of falls at her bungalow following John's funeral. One evening, when Mam and I went for our usual visit, we struggled to open the front door and were shocked to find that Nana was slumped against it. We had assumed that she had fallen over once again and just couldn't get back up, but it only took us a few minutes to realise that something more serious was going on.

As it turned out, Nana had been having heart problems and it was possible the falls that she had been having were actually mini strokes. As we went into 1991, Nana started to deteriorate and she was admitted to hospital. It all happened so quickly that we were convinced she'd started to give up on life. We did our best to make things bearable for her, tidying her bungalow and making things more comfortable for her.

But I had something else on my mind too. I started to feel really unwell. I'd been experiencing severe pains in my stomach and they were becoming very persistent. Something went off in my mind – I still don't know what it was – but I became convinced that my coil might have disappeared. I obsessed over it for weeks, realising that I could no longer feel it. Was this what was causing my pain?

I made an appointment to see a nurse. I wanted her to reassure me that everything was fine, but she asked me if I might be pregnant.

'I can't be,' I insisted, panic rising up in my chest. 'Not unless my coil has come out. I need to know if it's still there.'

'Well, look, I'll check,' she told me, setting me up for the examination. 'But it's worth me pointing out that I've delivered many a baby with the coil in their little hands.'

I felt sick at the thought of this. So maybe I was pregnant? Maybe that was what had me in complete agony? And if so, why? That shouldn't happen, should it?

I couldn't help myself. I hurried home and bought a pregnancy test on the way. All the while I tried my hardest to work out my dates and realised that maybe my period was actually a little late. I'd put it down to my worry about Nana and my continuing grief; my cycle was sometimes affected by stress. I took the test and some part of me knew the result before it was confirmed.

I was pregnant. My heart sank as the blue line appeared – the blue line that I really didn't want to see. *Oh my God, this is so unfair*, I thought. I had a coil; this shouldn't have been happening. It wasn't the right time to have a baby.

I was still in agony and decided to tell the doctors I'd taken a test. I was terrified that I was having an ectopic pregnancy. As it turns out they were worried about it too, as I soon found myself back in the hospital waiting to have a scan.

Every time the word 'pregnancy' was mentioned, I felt sick. I was even more mortified when the scan confirmed that I was about six weeks pregnant. To be truthful, Peter and I were gutted. I had my nana in hospital poorly and we were only weeks away from our wedding. Peter was in training for a new job and so money was tight for him, and I'd only just started a new job myself. Why now?

And so we had a difficult decision to make. Dad was working away from home and so Peter and I confided in my mam, hoping she could advise us. But ultimately it was mine and Peter's choice. And that choice was to have an abortion.

I need to say now that it was far from an easy decision. I was conflicted and confused and couldn't get a handle on my emotions. I wanted to know why I had been in such pain all this time, which was now strangely subsiding. The doctors hadn't found anything wrong and had suggested that it might have been trapped wind. I wasn't convinced: I knew something was wrong.

Or did I? Maybe in actuality I was looking for a reason not to go ahead with the pregnancy. We weren't ready for children. I didn't want to disappoint my parents, but it was just the wrong time. It hadn't been that long since I'd had a full-on mental breakdown after a break-up; I wasn't sure I was mentally strong enough to cope with having a baby when I'd been through so much turmoil. What use would I be as a mother if I went crazy after I'd given birth?

I cried so much, constantly second-guessing myself. I think it helped a lot that Peter seemed to feel the same way. Babies hadn't featured in our plans for the near future, and we were stressed enough with planning the wedding and the uncertainty of not knowing if Nana would pull through.

And so we went ahead. I knew it was the right choice, and I wanted to act immediately while I still felt sure.

My consultant, however, was really unhappy with our choice and he made no attempt to hide his feelings. He didn't want to listen to the fact that I had been seriously ill in the past and that the stress of my situation was causing my anxiety to come back with a vengeance. What if the depression followed suit? I just wasn't prepared for that.

But it elicited no sympathy whatsoever from him. He plonked my file down hard on the desk, virtually throwing it at me. 'Fine. If that's what you have decided, that's it then,' he said, with genuine disgust in his voice. He made me feel terrible about the entire thing – suddenly I felt two inches tall. It wasn't my fault! I'd been using precautions! I'd been on the coil! I honestly thought that the only way I could possibly have become pregnant was if the coil had fallen out, not when it was perfectly intact!

If we couldn't feel protected with a coil, then what hope did any of us have?

I left the appointment feeling heartbroken. I felt bad enough as it was, without being made to feel any worse by a professional who was supposed to help me. I wasn't offered any counselling either – but maybe that was because I wanted to rush through the process.

While I waited for the appointment for my termination, we carried on visiting Nana Lizzie in hospital. It soon became clear that she wouldn't be returning to her bungalow, bless her, as she was deteriorating quickly. She had fallen out of her bed, which angered Mam so much. She was convinced that Nana Lizzie was being neglected in hospital.

But as much as Mam wanted to place the blame on them, there was no escaping the truth: Nana no longer wanted to be here. She'd stopped taking her tablets. It was obvious she'd never come home to her bungalow again. Life without our John was too much for her: the day he was killed was the day a light went out in Nana's life.

In the early hours of 30th April 1991, less than a year after we lost John, we received a phone call from the hospital telling us that Nana didn't have long to live. Mam, Susan, and I all jumped into a taxi and rushed off to be by her side. It was about 4am when we arrived, but the scene awaiting us was horrible. Nana was on an oxygen machine and it was just about keeping her alive. We all huddled around her side and held her hands.

Susan began to sob silently. She was still mourning the tragic loss of her beautiful young son, and now she was about to lose Nana Lizzie. Nana had been such an important part of her life as she had been the one who had brought her up during her teenage years. Mam looked small and weak in her grief, terrified at the prospect of losing her mother. And I sat there next to them, wondering how I was supposed to cope with another bereavement on top of everything I was going through. I wasn't sure how much more my mind could take.

I could feel a cold, dark depression seeping into my psyche, and I knew it was something more than grief. But by then I'd become an expert at tamping down my emotions, and I pulled myself together in order to be there for my mam and Susan. Our family was tiny enough and our main anchor in it was leaving us behind. We stayed with her for the rest of the night, until slowly she faded away and took her final breaths.

We were united in our grief but part of me still felt apart from the rest of my family because I had to keep my own personal sadness to myself. Mam obviously knew about our problems but Peter and I had sworn her to secrecy. It was a looming problem and I didn't want anyone else to have to cope with it.

Fate can be cruel as well as kind. My termination was booked for the day before Nana's funeral. I was only a matter of weeks pregnant, but back then I still needed an operation rather than taking a pill. I've blocked the entire ordeal from my mind; I can barely remember any of it. All I can really recall is coming back around to a lovely, hot cup of tea. I felt numb and didn't particularly feel sad or traumatised. In all honesty the only thing I think I felt was relief. This way I could just get on with my life, with dealing with my grief and trying to get my mental health back on track. I craved normality again.

Getting through the funeral the next day was hard. I was tired and very sore from the operation, and I felt angry and victimised by the world. Part of it was selfish, too. I was getting married in just four weeks. Why couldn't Nana have hung on till then? Why had I had to go through an abortion during a time that was supposed to be the most romantic of my life? The bad news had just bombarded me over the past few years and months and it felt like I was hanging onto any kind of happiness by a thread.

But my wedding was coming up. Surely that would make everything better. Wouldn't it?

CHAPTER 11
What Had I Done?

It was 1991, and surely now, after all the heartache that we had been through, we were due a little bit of happiness in our lives. Our wedding seemed the perfect opportunity to cheer ourselves up, make a positive commitment and let our hair down. It had taken me an awful lot of planning; I'd enjoyed it. It proved to be a helpful distraction and as a bit of a perfectionist, it suited me fine. I had literally taken care of every last detail except for the men's suits. I left that to them; they knew what they had to do.

Soon the big day arrived and everything went like a dream. The service was beautiful; it was even likened to a royal wedding! I guess it was all very fancy, but having a day of celebration together, rather than one of sadness, was like a soothing salve over a healing emotional wound. What made it particularly special was Dad's speech. He spoke so highly of me, his beautiful daughter, who had made him incredibly proud. I blinked back tears as he spoke. This was the first time he'd ever told me how much I meant to him. It didn't erase all the trauma that had gone on before, but it helped a little to know how he really felt. I was a 23-year-old girl hearing my dad's approval for the first time.

Our honeymoon was a week away in Jersey. We had a great time, despite the fact that I was still suffering from the recent operation I'd had. I thought I had only the physical symptoms as I was a blissful newly wed. But now, when I look back at the photographs, I realise that in some of them I look quite sad. I guess there's only so much you can wallpaper over internal damage.

Even now that I was married, we continued to live with Mam and Dad. Dad was still working away and when he returned home at the weekends we would socialise together. By this time things were looking good for me at work as I'd been promoted to Housing Benefit Officer, the same grade as the other staff. I had a lot of job satisfaction in that post, as it meant that I was interviewing and engaging with the public. I also had increased responsibilities, which added to my sense of worth and made me feel like I was contributing to society. A little part of me was still that young girl looking for validation. Peter undertook some training to work towards a career. I trusted him wholeheartedly to provide for our future.

The year continued and all was well. It was a strange Christmas with no Nana Lizzie any more, as she had always come around to ours for her lunch. I missed her wonderful smile and infectious laugh, and more than a few times I wished she was still there sitting with us, drinking a few sherries. We managed to get through the day despite our grief, because we had no other choice.

But all too soon it seemed like I was due another downfall. One night in bed I lifted my head from my pillow. Nothing in particular prompted me. I just felt the urge to do it. It was then that I experienced a beautiful vision. The only way I can describe is that it was like looking through a kaleidoscope and seeing an array of beautiful, shimmery colours. I felt so elated and joyful that I shot up in bed, shaking Peter awake. I tried to tell him what had just happened but he was still half-asleep and too tired to understand anything I was saying.

My excitement was short-lived, though. A different feeling hit me: a pang of guilt. I closed my eyes as the negative emotion crept over me and I could see tiny little coffins running through my mind. Terrified, I tried my hardest to blot it out and go back to sleep.

The following day my behaviour become even more erratic and strange. I told my parents and Peter that I had had an epiphany.

'I've been spiritually uplifted,' I said, my tone deadly serious. I then started quoting the Bible.

Why was I doing this? Even though I'm Catholic, I had never sat around reading out Bible passages.

Things became even weirder. I was absolutely convinced that I couldn't die. I'd become invincible, I told Peter. He took me out for a walk to clear my head and to calm me down, but all it did was encourage me. 'If I walk out into that road,' I began, 'Nothing will happen to me. Even if I got hit by a car, I would never be killed.'

Peter was bewildered and terrified in equal measure. He had no idea what had come over me. I didn't question it myself; it all made perfect sense to me. We carried on walking and I insisted we visit Uncle Barry. Why? So I could tell him I'd seen Nana in my vision, of course!

But there's no way Barry was ever going to accept this, even if he was willing to take me seriously. He wasn't a big believer in anything himself and told me, in no uncertain terms, that what I was saying was crackers. My response to this was to leave his house and sprint all the way home, with poor Peter trying his hardest to keep up with me. An abnormal level of energy was coursing through me. I can't explain it any more clearly than to say I felt that I was running *outside* of my body. Peter was beside himself. Nothing he could say or do could snap me back into reality or make me start acting normally.

Things did not improve over the next few weeks. I was hit with an overwhelming feeling of loss. One night I ran around to my nana's house, but of course there was no real sense in that. She'd passed away the year before. But something in my mind hadn't accepted that. It was too much for my mentally ill brain to compute, and so it was like I'd rewound time somehow. I also felt as though I should be preparing for the arrival of a baby – a baby, of course, that would have been due to be born around this time. I was nesting, and wanted everything to be ready for my baby. But of course, no baby was coming.

The termination was playing on my conscience, and so Peter and I made an appointment to see our local priest. I don't know what I wanted from this – forgiveness, maybe? Nothing about my thinking was rational at this point. I started to argue with Peter on the way to the appointment, blaming him for the decision I'd made. This kind of conflict was too difficult for the priest to handle. He was unsure of what to say to me, and so his solution was to drive me to the home of a local lady who was anti-abortion. She thought it was important to save babies' lives. Looking back on this, I still cannot fathom why the priest thought this was a good idea. This was clearly the worst move that could have been made for me, and it was not to be without consequences.

On arriving at her house I was so in need of comfort that I just allowed her to hold me like a child. She was getting on a bit, but her embrace was strong and firm and I needed it. She had a kind face and a pretty smile. I trusted her instantly. I was past worrying about boundaries and still in a delusional state. In my eyes this woman was the mother of God and was going to take away my sin and my pain.

She sat with me into the small hours, discussing my termination and asking me if the baby had been Peter's. I was quite shocked that she could even ask me that question, but she just couldn't understand why I had made the decision for any other reason. I was baffled as to why she'd even thought that I could have slept with someone else. We clearly didn't know how to understand each other.

At some point during the night she placed a model of a tiny baby in my hand and told me that that was what I had lost. I felt something in my heart break irreparably. She then told me that I would come to know the sex of my baby, and that sometime soon I should write a letter to him or her and ask for forgiveness.

'You should also name the baby,' she told me, her hand on my shoulder. 'But never name a future child the same name, as it is theirs only.'

I hung onto her every word. I saw no reason to question anything she was telling me to do. She was God's mother, of course, so she was the best person to tell me what I should do. I broke down in tears but over my own wretchedness. What had I done?

I left that woman's house in a far worse state than when I'd arrived. Peter was at his wits' end. I carried on talking nonsense to myself and to anyone that would listen that night, often babbling incoherently. I scared Peter so much that he took me the hospital, desperate for some kind of help.

But none was to come. I was given some tablets to help me sleep, and was sent on my way. Was it any wonder I was declining so rapidly?

The tablets did nothing to help. I couldn't sleep that night or the following one. A distant family member had come to visit us – I'll be damned if I could remember who it was – and I exhausted myself talking to them until the early hours. It wasn't a smart move, because the lack of sleep made me feel like I was breaking in two. I could feel myself losing my mind.

A couple of nights later we were sitting and watching an old video of Dad's. It was a Daniel O'Donnell music video. My Dad worshipped him, and I adored him too. Things were pretty normal to begin with; we were all singing along to the music and enjoying each other's company. Until it happened.

Suddenly I felt a very strange feeling taking my place in my tummy. I could feel it rising. I could clearly see my tummy getting bigger and bigger. *I know what this is*, I thought. I was going to have my baby!

Oh my goodness, I felt so excited. I knew what I had to do. I proceeded to lie down on the floor, legs open and pulled up, waiting for the impending labour.

Poor Mam was horrified at what she was seeing. As I continued to work through my 'labour' she called the ambulance. I think she was slightly hysterical at this point. I can understand why.

A truly heartbreaking part of this was that when the ambulance arrived, I was only too willing to get in because I felt very excited. I was convinced I would return with a newborn baby.

As we drove towards the hospital, I lost my grip on reality very quickly. Peter held my hand as I stared up at the ambulance ceiling. I started seeing flashes, like little bolts of lightning. I had no idea what they were but they made me happy. I vaguely remember coming to the realisation that it wasn't actually physically possible to be having a baby, but I made up my mind that it was some sort of miracle. God wanted this for me.

God knows what I must have looked like. I bet the paramedics were baffled at what was going on. I looked such a fool as I was wearing a beautiful pair of khaki culottes with a matching jacket and a very pretty top underneath. This all was absolutely fine, until you arrived at my feet where I was wearing huge doggy slippers. You know, the ones you can buy around Christmas time. I both looked *and* acted like I was completely crazy.

I also remember sitting in front of a female doctor and answering lots and lots of questions. This was very exciting and glamorous. It was obvious to me that she was writing an article on me, maybe for the newspaper or a local magazine, talking all about me and the miracle that was unfolding in front of her. It didn't occur to me that she was actually a consultant trying to establish why I had lost my mind.

Following this little interview, I was admitted to a hospital bed. A huge smile was plastered across my face as I prepared myself for giving birth to my baby. They gave me some drugs to knock me out, and when I came around five nurses surrounded my bed. I relayed the good news to them.

A cacophony of noise hit me as the nurses scrambled over each other to yell at me that I wasn't pregnant.

'Did you think for even a minute that your tummy is one of a nine months' pregnant woman?' one of them sneered at me. 'You are *not* having a baby. Stop this nonsense.'

Now, I appreciate that the nurses were having to deal with very difficult circumstances that day. But I know I deserved better than to be treated in that manner. It felt like bullying, and there must have been a better way to deal with me, even back then when mental illness was not as well understood. One of the problems for people with mental health issues is that people often assume we do not know what we are saying. Well, I can't speak for everyone but I know that in my case I always knew what I was saying. I just didn't realise *why* I was saying it. To me, it was obvious that I was about to give birth to a miraculous baby. I didn't have any idea that I was having a breakdown. It cannot be just taken for granted that someone who is poorly doesn't have a clue what they're talking about. Often they do. Their words make sense, especially in the context of what's going through their mind. But it's the reality of the situation that they struggle with.

When they told me I wasn't having a baby, it triggered a deep, feral anger within me. I started to become distressed, and that's when they all, collectively, tried to pin me down on bed. I tried to fight them off. In the scuffle I accidentally struck one poor nurse and broke her glasses. I then suffered a grand mal seizure.

All this time, poor Peter was observing this in the background feeling extremely helpless and so sad watching his wife go through this. He did say to me some time later that he would never forget the look on my face, the look of sheer terror. As I blacked out I must have caught my tongue, as Peter told me later that blood seeped out of the side of my mouth. It must have been like a horror movie.

I stayed in hospital for exactly seven days. I still felt religious, but I'd pulled myself out of the baby delusion. I was shaky and felt weak and fragile. I couldn't quite come to terms with what had happened to me.

During my stay I was friendly with the odd lovely member of staff, but I remained wary of the ones who had treated me so badly. The nurse whose glasses I had broken couldn't stop mentioning it and she was convinced I didn't remember what I'd done.

'Actually, I do remember,' I told her angrily. 'And I would still punch anyone who was forcing me down onto a bed against my will!'

It was plain to see that we were not going to get on at all and so I tried my hardest to completely ignore her. I made friends with a few of the other girls there. One of the girls told me all about her plans to marry her partner when she was better. She explained how difficult it would be as her funds were low. In the spirit of generosity I told her that I could help her out if she wanted me to, by letting her borrow my wedding dress. After all, I wasn't going to be needing it again and it was only sitting in my wardrobe gathering dust. She was so grateful and excited about this that she went on to tell one of the nurses.

'It would be a good idea not to take any notice of her,' the nurse whispered to the girl. 'She's mentally unwell and she's probably only saying that. Once she's better I doubt it'll happen.'

My face grew hot and my chest heaved. How dare she be so patronising? It wasn't in my nature to keep quiet, and so I told her that her attitude towards mentally ill people was appalling.

I knew the staff found me irritating. I truly believe that is because I had a voice and, unlike some patients who were too poorly to be able to speak up, I wasn't quiet. Ill or not, I was not going to be silenced. I'm pretty sure I was sent home at 8pm one evening because they had heard enough from me. They didn't give me any further diagnosis. They didn't explain to me why my mind had done what it had done. They just let me back out to fend for myself against my own mind.

It didn't seem a very appropriate time to discharge a mental health patient, but that's what they did, with no complaints from me. I was quite happy to get myself a taxi and head home. It seems quite amazing that the hospital could slam a section on me for a week and then decide just like that to send me home. How times have changed!

It would take some time before I realised that the trauma of my termination had triggered this psychotic episode. It took me a while to open up to people and tell them what I'd been through. I needed people's support and help in order to heal, but of course they could only give me these things when I let go of the secret that I had kept bottled up for so long. Only then could my friends and colleagues help me through my ordeal. I came to the personal conclusion that my decision hadn't been the right one after all, otherwise it wouldn't have affected me so horrifically.

In the most traumatic way possible, I'd come to realise that I really did want a baby after all.

CHAPTER 12

Finding a Purpose

During my stay in hospital I had noticed an advert for a break at a hotel in the Lake District. *Are You Feeling Depressed?* it asked readers.

Well, that definitely sounded like me. And a break in the Lake District sounded great to me, after all that I had been through. Peter agreed, and so that January we hired a car and went off for our weekend.

It took an awful long time to get there. I started to become a bit disheartened. At one point in the journey I suggested that it might be better to find somewhere a little closer. But Peter insisted – if the hotel I'd seen in the advertisement was in the Lake District, then that was where I had to go.

The advert had sold the hotel as a lovely little cosy place, full of warmth and charm. It was set back in the middle of nowhere but surrounded by beautiful scenery. I guess nowadays people would describe the appeal of the place as something to do with mindfulness. The owner had two of my favourite breeds of dog: a standard Poodle and a lovely golden Labrador. They made me smile and lifted my spirits.

My little weekend away did me good. I felt well-rested and at ease, as though I'd run away from my anxiety for a bit. When I got back, my friends from work surprised me with some flowers and a teddy bear. They'd heard about how poorly I'd been and wanted to show their support. I almost cried then and there. Mental illness was such a taboo subject at the time and it meant so much to me that I hadn't scared anyone off.

I confided in one of the girls, Sue, about how harrowing my experience had actually been.

'We'd all realised that you weren't really yourself last year,' she told me candidly, holding my hand.

I knew then that, even before my psychotic episode, I hadn't dealt with my termination as well as I thought I had. Sue was brilliant. She couldn't understand why I hadn't felt able to talk about my problems with her or the other girls, especially since we all got along so well. But I'd felt ashamed. We'd both been brought up in strict Catholic families and when I explained my guilt and embarrassment to her, she seemed to get it.

'You don't have to deal with this sort of thing on your own any more,' she reassured me. 'We're all in this together.'

I sighed a huge sigh of relief. Somehow just this simple gesture made everything so much easier. I wished that I hadn't bottled things up now; in hindsight it had only made things harder for me. It is so true, what they say: a problem shared is a problem halved. If only all people with mental health issues knew this.

Before long we had some very surprising news: I was pregnant again. I was stunned, but this time in a completely different way. I thought it was just amazing news. Here was my opportunity to finally get things right.

While we still lived with my parents, I was determined to make this work. I felt that I had been given a second chance. I longed for this baby in a way that I hadn't before. I was still a bit worried about telling Dad, even though me and Peter were married. Maybe it was because

I knew he would worry about us not having enough money to look after a family. But I couldn't let myself worry about that. Perhaps I didn't want to.

Despite everything I'd been through, my family were thrilled for me. It was a bonus that Peter was due to go on a work placement alongside his training. While my immediate plan was to just enjoy my pregnancy and take extra care of myself, I knew how determined I was to return to work. My occupational therapist didn't think this was a good idea.

'Look, you've just been through a mental breakdown,' he said to me, clearly concerned. 'I really don't think you should go back, at least until you're twelve weeks pregnant. But to be honest I think the best course of action for you would be to leave on the grounds of ill health.'

I admit I was shocked at this suggestion. I was used to just gritting my teeth and getting on with it after a setback and was really surprised that other people didn't feel the same way. I went against his recommendations and threw myself back into work.

I soon realised, though, that this was a mistake. By the time I went back my team had moved buildings, a move which had been on the cards for some time. I had hoped to have been a part of it, as a move of office is a big thing. But my breakdown had put a stop to that. Everyone else was settled in their new surroundings and here I was, feeling like a spare part, late to the party. It felt exactly like starting senior school again, when everyone else had settled in before I'd had a chance to get started. And as much as everyone tried to make me feel welcome I just couldn't get back into the swing of it. There were more new rules to learn regarding benefits and I just couldn't take it all in. I felt overwhelmed and powerless to do anything about it.

I was due to see my occupational health doctor again and I started to think back to the conversation we had regarding me leaving work on the grounds of ill health. Work was becoming stressful for everyone as cutbacks started to kick in and workloads were growing ever bigger. The warning signs stared me square in the face and I could feel those familiar feelings of depression and anxiety crawling their way back again, bit by bit, every single day. Fear gripped me.

Remember how you've dealt with stress before, Karen, I thought to myself. Was I really ready to risk another breakdown while pregnant? Of course I couldn't. I couldn't bear the thought. And so I made the decision not to return to work.

Even just making the decision was a huge relief. As Peter was now earning money, we bought our first car. It was so exciting! A real taste of freedom. I also felt more content being at home, knowing that I was free from the stresses of my job.

But it was still important that we found a home preferably before the birth of our baby. We had considered buying a house but at the last minute decided that was not going to be the best option, especially considering my mental health and the uncertainty of Peter's future work. Dad also didn't want me to have the worry about trying to pay a mortgage with the threat of losing a home hanging over me. He suggested that we rent instead.

But that was easier said than done. My name had been on the council's waiting list, for a flat, since I was 17. I had also informed the council a while back that I'd been sharing my bedroom with my husband. We now had to contact them to make them aware of our impending arrival. When they us at home, they told me they couldn't see any problem with me sharing a small box bedroom with my husband and our future child.

I couldn't believe the stupidity of their decision. I knew then that I had to tell them about my mental illness, which meant that they would have to contact my GP. I was so nervous about this, but I felt that it was worth a shot if it helped us to get our own home.

We had a really difficult task ahead of us. Convincing the local authority that we were in urgent need of accommodation was hard, but we had quite a number of people fighting our corner. It was refreshing to see so many people understanding and supporting my plight. It was lovely that they listened to me and understood that living with my parents in a very cramped home was affecting my mental health.

It's such a shame that the local authority couldn't recognise these issues themselves, though. Instead we had to contact a number of local councillors, our local MP, the doctor, and even the parish priest at one point. It was quite shocking that we had to go to such extreme lengths just to prove that mental illness was a real problem, and yet a single parent was actually allocated the house next door. I can only assume that they had more sympathy for her because whatever her problem was was either physical or more tangible than mental health issues.

I can only hope that as people are becoming more aware of mental health in today's day and age, that local authorities treat people with more dignity. As it was for us, it took a whole lot of time and energy before we received a call saying that a property had come up for us, right around the corner. It was ideal for us and didn't come a moment too soon, as the stress was seriously getting to me.

We were really excited until we were shown inside. The place was a mess. My heart sank into my shoes and I walked around the place in a huff, stomping my feet. Had we really waited all that time, and gone through all that grief, for this? Tears prickled at my eyes. I was so bloody tired of being disappointed all the time.

'Karen, relax,' Mam told me, taking hold of both my arms. 'Stop looking at it for what it is right now. They still need to refurbish the place and make it liveable anyway. Instead of looking at the mess, picture it as a lovely home. Picture what it *could* be.'

I saw her point, but it wasn't easy. Emotion was clouding my judgment. I had no other option though; my hands were tied. I knew fine well if we did not accept this property things would be very difficult for us. The decision was effectively made for us.

My new neighbour was delighted. She'd been worrying who was going to be living next door to her and so when she heard it was us she was very happy. It turned out that the previous tenants had been an elderly couple, and the renovation was going to take a lot of work. For some reason, I felt better when I learnt that the old couple had been religious. I had no idea why it meant so much to me. Other than during my psychotic episode, I wasn't overly religious in my own behaviour. Maybe it's because it reminded me of my late Nana Maisie, God love her. Her house had also been in much need of tender loving care when she had passed away.

The hard work commenced, and the first thing we did was to get rid of all the rubbish. We stripped the walls, which was insanely hard work, because they'd been coated with this horrific thick wallpaper. The more work we did the more we realised how much it was all going to cost. I wanted it to be perfect, but it'd come at a price.

'Once you put the kettle on, it will feel like home,' Dad winked. 'Just have a bit of patience.'

But my desire for a perfect home was costing a lot of money, and unwisely I racked up a bit of a debt on it. On reflection, I realise that I didn't need to have the best of everything right then and there, but that's how I felt at the time. I felt a compulsion to spend on the house quite unlike I'd ever done before and I whipped myself up into a bit of a spending frenzy. The debts mounted up but it was of no consequence to me: I just had a drive to buy nice things for my pretty new home. That was all that mattered to me at the time.

Trying to get it so perfect took a lot of time, too, and soon it became apparent that things might not be finished before the baby arrived. I'd got so carried away, insisting that even the garden had to be sorted before we moved in. We even moved the cot into my bedroom at Mam's just in case.

Eventually Peter managed to convince me that I was, quite frankly, being a bit crazy. He did his best to show me what was most important. It was time, in his eyes, to just get over it and move in. After all, it wasn't helping that we were now paying the rent as well as paying Mam board money for living with her.

Reluctantly I agreed. We had lots of lovely furniture and all our essentials anyway, so it was easy to just move in. It still looked beautiful compared to how it was originally. My anxiety gave way to pride. We'd done it.

I was all prepared, our home was ready, the cot was in place, and now I just needed someone to fill it. My pregnancy had gone extremely well with no real health issues bar my anxiety. My little one was actually overdue by the time I felt my first contraction. To the point that I was actually a little late. I felt brilliant, and all I wanted now was for this much longed-for baby.

Finding out the sex of the baby before it's born wasn't the done thing then. And so it wasn't until I had my beautiful, blonde, blue-eyed boy on that cold winter's day in 1992 that I knew what fate had held in store for me (although I'd had my suspicions). We named him Peter Anthony. It was one of the best days of my entire life.

I cried tears of joy. This might sound strange but in that moment when I first held him, I felt like something in me had been healed. Peter Anthony couldn't ever have replaced the baby I'd had aborted, but I still couldn't help feeling as though I'd been given my baby back. Like I'd solved a great wrongness in my life.

I stayed in hospital for a few days. That was the rule back then, when the baby was your first born. I was grateful for it though; it gave me time to bond with my baby without everyone being around. It also helped me adjust to the monumental change that had just happened in my life, as the nurses were there to help. He suffered with projectile vomiting and didn't take his milk very well, and so the added support was invaluable. I was so grateful to them.

I begged the staff to let me go home the evening before my fifth day, which was Bonfire Night. It was a strange feeling, leaving the hospital. I felt so protective of my new baby. Even getting into the car and fastening him into his car seat made me feel very nervous. I wanted us to drive ever so slowly as we had precious cargo on board. The short ride home felt so nerve-wracking – especially with it being Bonfire Night; there were lots of cracks and bangs. The relief was immense when we eventually arrived home.

That night I stayed at home and just stared, constantly, at my new baby boy in his Moses basket. I was overwhelmed with love. I had been through so much trauma to get here, but I was finally a mum. I hoped to God that I could stay mentally well for him. I had a reason to fight now.

This baby was going to be so loved!

CHAPTER 13
It's Never as Easy as You Think

The next few years brought a feeling of contentment and pride. I loved every part of being a mum. I became quite regimented and domesticated; I wanted to be the perfect wife and mother. I loved my new home, the one I'd spent so much to achieve, and wanted it to look nice. I had rotas for my cleaning and a cooked tea ready every evening for Peter. I'd achieved a new kind of adult life and I thrived on it.

It wasn't perfect, of course; Peter Anthony did give me reasons to worry. He continued to throw up his milk and he struggled to put on weight. This made me worry. A LOT. Often I convinced myself that there was something seriously wrong with him. Shouldn't he have just fed naturally, like the books had told me? Family and friends reassured me that it was normal, but I couldn't stop the anxiety tormenting me every time I tried to feed him.

The fear never truly disappeared entirely. Many times, Peter would get home after work to find me slumped on the floor in tears. Even when my baby's oesophagus grew stronger and he stopped vomiting, my distress didn't let up. The sleepless nights continued as he started to teethe, and even that took far longer than many other babies. Was I a failure? Could I handle yet another long, drawn-out process where I would become increasingly impatient?

I tried my best, though, to be as happy as possible. After all, I'd achieved my dream of becoming a mother. I loved this so much that it actually wasn't that long before I'd decided to have another baby. I remembered my own childhood and how lonely I often felt with no brothers or sisters around. Life hadn't been easy for me for that reason. My husband had also grown up as an only child, and he felt the same way as me.

'Let's do it,' Peter smiled one night as I tentatively broached the subject. 'Let's give him a brother or sister.' I squeezed his hand and smiled back at him, delighted. Time to complete my perfect family.

And so, less than two years after our son was born, and after only trying for a few months, I discovered I was pregnant with our second child. We were absolutely thrilled. I think one or two people were surprised at how quickly we were to have another child, especially considering I'd struggled a little bit emotionally with Peter Anthony. But what did we have to lose? What did we have to wait for? It made perfect sense to do it now, while we were still young.

We celebrated Peter Anthony's second birthday and then waited with anticipation for our unborn baby to arrive. She was due on 25th November but was a few days late in arriving. By this time I was irritable and blamed everybody else for everything. I had a false alarm on the Saturday evening when Mam was convinced that I was in labour, but on arrival at the hospital it was confirmed that I wasn't. Not even a little bit. And yet, they still decided it was a good idea for me to stay overnight, just in case. I hated hospitals for obvious reasons. I was livid.

'Cheers for this,' I sneered at Mam. 'I just love being surrounded by women whose babies have already arrived.'

In my defence, I was incredibly uncomfortable! I was sent home on the Sunday and it wasn't until Monday tea time that the first contraction arrived. Mam came over to look after our Peter and I explained to him what was happening in the best way you can to a two-year-old.

Looking back, I can already see the signs that my emotions were all over the place and a bit unstable. But when you're heavily pregnant, you put it down to that. My labour was progressing really well when the nurses decided to give me diamorphine. This was fine until the midwife started checking the monitor, looking unsure of herself.

'What, what is it?' I asked her frantically, my eyes jumping from her expression to the monitor and back again. 'What's wrong?'

'Nothing's wrong,' the nurse reassured me, touching my hand briefly in a comforting manner. 'I'm just going to get the doctor.' And off she went to fetch him.

I burst into tears. 'What's happened to my baby?' I wailed at the midwife, who looked rather taken aback at my distress.

'Shh, it's fine!' she reassured me. 'The diamorphine has just made your baby fall asleep. The nurse is just getting the doctor to confirm it so we know how to proceed.'

Relief flooded over me and I shed a few more tears. I needed to get a grip on myself, but no sooner had I done that than the labour started.

For some bizarre reason, I'd always been convinced that our baby would be born on the 28th November, and during my labour I was pushing myself to give birth on the right date! I have no idea why. I can't really explain my thought processes at this point. But it turns out I was right – at one minute to midnight, with no time to spare, our baby came into the world.

'You have had a baby girl,' the midwife announced, beaming. She placed my gorgeous girl on my chest and I cried once again. This time I was overwhelmed with how lucky I felt. I had a beautiful daughter to complete my dream family.

The hospital experience was very different to when I gave birth to Peter Anthony. I was left lying in bed until almost 3.00am before staff came back to clean me up and put me into some fresh nightwear. It was horrible, uncomfortable and a bit embarrassing. Definitely not the way I wanted to spend the first few hours of my new baby's life.

Peter was then sent home and I was advised to try to get some sleep while they looked after my baby for me. Which sounds fine, but she cried constantly that night and I could hear her from my bed. It didn't seem right to sleep when my baby needed me. The nurses tried to get me to rest, telling me that she'd be all mine in the morning. But it didn't make any sense to me, and I couldn't get to sleep. I watched the clock go round and round, feeling shattered but unable to do anything else. I couldn't wait to get out of there – it took the shine off my happiness and I was sick of being there already.

When we got home, my parents were waiting for us. Dad asked me to name the baby Bernadette. I loved the name. What a lovely idea, for him to name his granddaughter. We called her Bernadette Marie, as Marie was my middle name. She was absolutely beautiful and I was completely in love.

But Bernadette's first few months weren't easy. Things were harder for us financially now that I wasn't working, and because Peter did contract work he was currently unemployed.

Things were going to be harder for us as by now I had left work completely after retiring on ill health and sadly Peter was unemployed, which was often the case with contract work. I now knew exactly what Mam meant when she talked about always living in a 'feast or famine'! Sometimes we found ourselves with lots of money for a while, which we got a bit carried away with. And then all of a sudden, there'd be no work and no money coming in whatsoever. I knew we had to take care of the pennies, but with such a young family it wasn't easy.

After the issues I'd had with Peter Anthony, I'd had hoped that everything would run smoothly with Bernadette. A fair few mothers had assured me that no two babies were alike and so I expected everything to be much easier. If only that was the case. Bernadette kept us up all night with colic and I started to feel sorry for myself.

Bernadette would scream the house down all night. I tried everything to soothe her. I tried watering down her feed, giving her Infacol drops, giving her baby massages … but nothing seemed to work. There was just no pacifying her at all. Even the health visitor was at a loss for what to do. Bernadette's piercing screams continued and she kicked about in pain. It cut through me like a knife.

Sleep was completely impossible. No sooner had we put Bernadette down for her sleep than the crying would start again. My husband Peter and I were absolutely shattered. It felt like an assault on my body and my mind. The stress was relentless and we struggled to cope. We got no rest during the day and then everything got far worse at night, when the colic was the worst. We were getting to the point where we could no longer keep track of the three-hourly feeds as we tried hard to stay lucid and functioning. We just had to offer her the bottle to see if it was needed.

I wished more than anything that my parents would offer to help. I didn't have it in me to ask them, but I craved just one offer of a night off so I could catch up on sleep. They only lived around the corner but no help was forthcoming. I became very resentful and the sleeplessness began to take its toll on me. I could feel my mind bending under the pressure again.

One night it came to me like a flash of lightning: a deep-seated conviction that we were going to win the lottery. It wasn't a wish or a hope; I *knew* it was going to happen. Peter nodded if I ever mentioned it, too tired to argue with me or out-reason me with logic. And so my conviction continued.

Strangely enough though, this new-found knowledge didn't even enter my head when I started spending again. I bought everything and anything I wanted, without even considering the consequences. If I wanted something, I would have it. It was as simple as that. Life was hard; it was stressful and sleepless. And what better way to relax than to treat myself with a bit of retail therapy? And so on and on it went – I spent recklessly and constantly.

I also began to have hallucinations. One of them was particularly frightening. I was at my mam and dad's house one night while Peter had the baby at our own house. I just needed one night away from her, although it still hadn't occurred to them to offer to take the baby instead. But still, I was over at their house to sleep – perhaps that would help me function better. I got into bed alongside Mam as Dad was out and there was only one bed.

'What's going on?' Dad chuckled when he got home and walked into the bedroom. 'Nicking my bed, eh? Never mind, I'll go and sleep on the settee.'

I looked closely at his face. *That can't be right*, I thought. Probably the lamplight. I blinked a couple of times, but it was no good. He still looked the same. I immediately freaked out.

He looked like a corpse. His eyes were black and sunken and his face was pale and gaunt. I felt physically sick.

He left to go downstairs and I turned to Mam. 'Oh my God,' I said to her hysterically. 'Dad's got cancer.'

'What?' Mam asked, horrified. 'What are you talking about? What has he said?'

'He doesn't have to say anything,' I insisted. 'I just know. Dad has cancer!'

Mam shifted upwards in the bed, looking down at me with obvious concern on her face. 'Karen, it's fine. Nothing's wrong with him. You're just tired and stressed.'

But I was having none of it. I shot out of the bed like a scalded cat and rushed to put my clothes on. I just had to get out of there and go home. I had really frightened myself and I knew what I had seen. I ran down the stairs and Dad asked me what I was doing.

He was lying down on the couch. For some unfathomable reason this terrified me even more. He still looked deathly to me and I could barely look at him. I made up some excuse about the baby being unsettled and told him I had to go home.

'I never heard the phone,' he said in a sleepy voice. 'Eh, I don't know, you try your best for them.'

I couldn't listen to him any more. It was like talking to the walking dead. I whispered good night and fled the darkened room. I walked home as quickly as I could.

When I got home I crept to the landline, trying to not wake anyone up. There was actual silence for once and I was glad to hear that Peter was obviously managing to get some sleep. Immediately I dialled the Samaritans' number. I was so distressed. I just needed to talk to someone.

In floods of tears, I begged them to listen to me. I spent a considerable amount of time on the phone with one of their operators. They soothed me and tried to reassure me, even telling me that they thought I'd had a premonition. Feeling vilified but still scared, I came off the phone. I tried my hardest to get some much-needed sleep.

When my health visitor next visited, I confided in her that I was struggling to cope. I didn't feel my usual self and I felt seriously low and weepy. I knew I didn't have post-natal depression as I'd looked it up and didn't have any of the symptoms. But my feelings *were* worryingly familiar.

'I've had this before,' I cried to the health visitor. 'It's the depression I get when I'm sleep deprived. I've been hospitalised for this in this past.' I was so scared.

Thankfully the health visitor recognised my symptoms. She told me to visit my GP, who put me on lithium. He was convinced that I had manic depression. I have to say that I'm glad he prescribed me this drug. It was one of the quickest recoveries I had ever experienced. Over the next two or three weeks, Peter did his best to hold the fort while I rested. I felt myself growing stronger as I finally managed to get some sleep.

I wasn't really sure what on earth that night was all about, and I pushed it to the back of my mind. I was in no position to fall apart; I just had to try to cope as best I could.

In time, Bernadette recovered from her colic and we settled her into her bedtime routine. We still struggled for some time as Peter was still looking for work, but it was just as well he was at home a lot, because otherwise we'd never have survived what we'd gone through.

I still didn't manage to shake off my resentment. I wondered why we hadn't been given any help and it really hurt me, especially when we were always there for others. I came to realise that sometimes people are just too wrapped up in their own lives to actually consider what's going on with other people. I also knew that the type of issues I'd been having were difficult to understand. I knew deep down I would have to put these thoughts to the back of my mind – my parents were still my parents and I believed that I owed them my respect.

The GP referred me to a counsellor. It opened my eyes to the power of therapy. After all I'd gone through, it hadn't occurred to me that this was what I had been missing. But now that I was receiving it, it made total sense. I was mentally ill. Medicine could only do so much. It helped so much to talk about my experiences, my fear, my depression and my anxiety. I could open up about my strange convictions and hallucinations without fear of being branded a freak or a lunatic. I could talk to them about my bizarre spending habits and my tendency to break down in the face of conflict or hardship. It was incredibly cathartic to get it off my chest.

CHAPTER 14

A Premonition Comes True

As my relationship with my counsellor developed and my mental health improved, I thought that maybe I, too, should learn some counselling skills. And so I made the decision to enrol on a basic course and volunteer for the Samaritans. Going back to college felt great this time around as it felt like I was doing it for the right reasons. After I passed the basic course, I went on to work towards certification. I was enjoying my time at college and felt like I was part of something important.

As we approached our Bernadette's first birthday in 1995, we felt relieved and a sense of achievement that we'd survived the year. Things had been difficult both financially and emotionally, but our amazing little family made it all worth it. We believed deep down that our situation would improve one day. The main thing was that we had each other.

One evening Dad had called to see us all. It was a pleasant evening and it was nice to enjoy my dad's company. I'd been growing closer to him recently; the violence at home seemed to have calmed down and he'd become more mellow. It allowed me to appreciate who he was as a person rather than this horrific monster who beat up my mam.

As soon as he'd left, though, Peter asked me if I had noticed a change in my dad's voice. No, I hadn't, actually, but I made a point of listening intently to my dad the next day.

Peter was right. His voice had changed, and it had a kind of echo to it. I thought it best to mention it to Mam and Dad as certainly something wasn't right. He didn't seem to have a cold or anything and so I told him to get it checked. Perhaps it was a throat infection or something. He went to see his GP who decided to send him to the ear, nose, and throat infirmary in town to be seen by a consultant. I wasn't too concerned and forgot about it.

But a few nights later things changed. I will never forget the night that Mam called me. I was just clearing our teapots away when the phone rang.

'Karen,' Mam said, and I instantly knew something was very wrong. 'It's your dad. He's been to the hospital.' She breathed in deeply as she tried to compose herself. 'He has throat cancer.'

My blood ran cold. I actually wasn't sure I'd heard her right, until she repeated herself. Dad had throat cancer.

I'd never dreamt that it was going to be anything as serious as this. I was devastated. I was also seriously freaked out. I had predicted this was going to happen. It made me feel scared of my own mind. Cancer was such a scary word, but we didn't hear it almost as much then as we do now, and that's what terrified me so much.

It turned out that Dad hadn't wanted me to find out. He didn't want to worry us. But he did seem very positive. Apparently the consultant had told him that if he could walk away and never smoke again, there was a good chance that he could be cured. And so Dad made up his mind: his life was just too important to throw it away by smoking cigarettes. I had to admire his courage and his decision to quit; he had been smoking from the age of twelve. It wasn't an easy change to make.

I knew that it was vital that I stayed strong for him; Dad did not need me to get ill while he fought this dreadful disease. And so I did my utmost to stay positive. I needed to, for my own sanity.

The first step for treatment was radiotherapy. He had a lot of sessions at the hospital. I stepped in to support him at his appointments because Mam found them very hard to deal with. It was a long process, but I was determined to get through it. My counselling course at college really helped me muddle through. It strengthened my conviction that I could use my new-found skills to help others.

I had come to realise the importance of being able to talk to someone in a very private and supportive way. All of my college friends helped me to cope with what I was going through as well, which was invaluable. As part of the course we went away for two residential weekends which, although we had work to do, proved to be a huge help. I was able to take some time out to reflect on what was happening and deal with my panic and anxiety.

Dad was eventually given the all clear. He emerged from the doctor's appointment smiling from ear to ear. He told me he felt great and promised that he'd leave the cigarettes alone and take things easy.

I was absolutely thrilled for Dad, but I did still have some issues with him that I opened up to my friends at college about. Dad had never really praised me or told me how he felt about me, barring that one speech at my wedding. I wanted his affection and he'd never shown me any. I was terrified of losing him to cancer and I feared that if I did, things would be left unsaid. I hated the idea.

'Maybe you need to take him out for a drink, just you and him, and tell him all of this,' one of my friends suggested. 'It might do you both some good to speak alone.'

It was worth a shot, surely. And so I went for it. I took him out one night and opened up about how I felt. And while he didn't exactly wrap his arms around me and become all mushy, we did have a great night together, reminiscing. It helped that we enjoyed each other's company that night. I guessed that that was the best I could really hope for. He was clearly set in his ways.

A person's journey with cancer is rarely simple. Just when things seemed to be getting better, Dad discovered another little lump in his neck. We were all seriously worried, but we had full faith in the consultant, who didn't hesitate. He booked Dad in for an operation to have the lump removed. I stayed with Mam while he was in the hospital.

I can't really describe what was going on in my head at this point. I had a constant fog of anxiety and worry in my head, like a head cold I couldn't shake off. But this time none of it was about me, and I had to support my mam. She was distressed and needed my help. I stayed with her while Dad was in hospital and tamped down my own misery. She needed me to be strong for her, and once again I bore the weight of the world on my shoulders.

But my mind was under attack by stress once again. I couldn't shake off the feeling that Dad was going to die. I was convinced, now more than ever, that back on that horrific night I'd really had a premonition. This really was only going to end one way.

Peter and my children kept me going, but the only thing that really helped me was my counselling course. My classmates provided me with a very good support network. Each week after class they would talk to me about what I was going through. It gave me some desperately needed inner strength. I also kept a journal, as this was a required part of the course. Reflecting on my feelings was a good way of understanding how I was coping at the time.

But June 1996 was fast approaching and soon my course would be finished. I didn't know how I'd cope without those lovely people who had been there for me all this time. I was going to miss them all but I was also going to miss the distraction.

We had one final residential weekend away. One lovely classmate, Kevin, asked me why I was unusually quiet. I just gave him a non-committal reply. I think I was distancing myself a little as I knew it would soon be time for us to say our goodbyes to one another. I wasn't sure my mind could cope with a sudden separation and change. They hadn't done me any good in the past. It felt like I was mentally preparing for an onslaught of mental illness and I was trying my hardest to arm myself for the fight.

On our last evening together our tutor thought it would be a good idea if we all wrote descriptive words for each other on a little piece of paper and pass it around. It was such a lovely idea and I could feel a tear in my eye when I read what people had written about me. I felt like that little girl all over again: still thriving on people's positive opinions. I'd never lost that character trait. It still mattered to me, deeply, what people thought. And I admit it helped me. I still have that piece of paper today and it gives me great comfort, especially when life gets tough and I convince myself I'm a bad person.

I felt very lonely when I left the course. I didn't feel my usual self, either. It was like a link between me and the real Karen had been severed. Fear had created a barrier between me and my mentally healthy self and I could feel myself walking down that dark, dangerous path to depression once again.

Mam and Dad's silver wedding anniversary was coming up that August. Peter and I thought it would be a nice treat to send them on a trip to Ireland. But it wasn't to be. Dad was simply too ill.

I began to find comfort in Daniel O'Donnell's music. Dad loved him so much and even when he was ill we would often watch his music videos together. After a while I started watching them alone in my spare time. The music soothed my battered soul and I would cry to myself as I listened to it.

The videos made me fall in love with Ireland. It looked like such a beautiful and peaceful land, so different from the world of pain that

I currently lived in. It certainly looked like a great place to escape to. Dad loved the Irish people, and he'd told me more than a few times that our ancestors were Irish. His grandparents were from Cork and Tyrone and so he and I felt a deep connection with the place. I began to fantasise about being there and I felt solace whenever I thought about it. My love for Daniel O'Donnell deepened.

But this was more than a simple admiration. In fact, my love was becoming an obsession. Soon I could think of nothing else. It was on my mind all the time. I began to lose sleep again. Mam got the doctor out to me, trying to pre-empt another breakdown. He gave me pills to take in order to help me sleep. Mam tucked me up in bed and gave me Horlicks, begging me to promise her that I would catch up on sleep. I think she knew my triggers by this point too and knew she wouldn't be able to cope with an ill daughter as well as a poorly husband.

But it was no good. I couldn't sleep and when Mam left the room, I switched on the radio. I knew for a fact that someone on there wanted to get a message to me, but they couldn't get through. They couldn't tell me what I needed to hear.

I need to find out what they want to tell me, I thought. I needed to go somewhere else that was playing music. The club! I got dressed hastily and made my way to the local.

There was a group of line dancers in the concert room. I felt a strong compulsion to join them and headed over. They must have been absolutely baffled, but I paid no attention to their reactions. I tried to dance with them, but one of them took one look at the glazed look in my eyes and sensed that something was wrong. They tried to take me aside but I wasn't listening. I needed to hear the music and join them in the dancing. It was the only way I'd receive the message.

My memory of that night is hazy. At some point Mam and Peter appeared, distressed at my strange behaviour. They got me into an ambulance and took me to the local hospital. I had completely lost control of my mind. I was a danger to myself.

Within a few hours I was placed on the intensive care ward and was very unsettled. I continued to act bizarrely. In the centre of the ward there was an office with all glass windows. There was a number of doctors and nurses in there. They began to play the parts of people in my life. The doctor was my dad. The nurses were Susan and my nanas. I shouted out to them, asking them to join me at my bed and have a chat. Mam and Peter insisted that I was seeing things, but I paid them no heed. I knew who they were. Everything that went through my mind made perfect sense to me. It was them that didn't understand.

It wasn't long before I was discharged. This was a huge mistake, because I had only one thought on my mind and now I had a plan: I was going to Ireland!

CHAPTER 15

A Dream Turns into a Nightmare

On my return home I begged and pleaded with Peter to take me to Ireland. We still didn't have a lot of money, but I convinced him that we could afford to go for at least a few days.

Peter was beside himself. He had absolutely no idea what to do with me. But I didn't consider how he was feeling; it wasn't within my capabilities. Everything was about me – mental illness can be incredibly introspective, and can make you appear to be very selfish.

I can only imagine now, looking back, how appalling this was for Peter. It affected him massively but he had no one to turn to. And I just didn't care. It makes me feel very sad to think of that now, as I am – as my colleagues described me – a very loving, caring, and kind person. But at that point I was oblivious. I wanted to go to Ireland.

Peter knew I was still ill, but he couldn't convince the doctors that my medication wasn't working any more. I became increasingly demanding and in the end, he agreed that we could go, but not for very long. Perhaps he thought that it would placate me if I went for a quick visit. He knew deep down that I was obsessed with Ireland, though, and he was quite worried that I might never want to return. He decided that the trip would be very short.

Before we left for Ireland my behaviour became even more erratic and my temper flared. One day, as I was sitting opposite my dad in the living room, I started screaming at him.

'I hate you!' I screamed in his face. 'How *could* you? How could you?'

'How could I what?' he yelled back at me, looking so thin and vulnerable. The poor man had no idea what was going on.

I didn't answer him. I just curled up into the foetal position on the floor and continued to scream. It must have looked like a scene from *The Exorcist*! The anger hit me over and over again. Memories of Dad beating my mother up swirled around in my mind and I felt like a little child again. I was furious that he didn't understand my illness as well. I didn't care that he was ill, but at the same time I felt terror at the thought of losing him. I couldn't get a handle on my own thoughts.

Dad didn't deserve this. I know that. But logic and morality didn't play a part in that moment.

Somehow, miraculously, I managed to hoodwink my doctor into believing I was okay. I guess I was just so desperate to go to Ireland that I was able to lie well, and soon we were off.

My little ones were excited to be going away with us. They were far too young to understand that their mam was not well. They weren't to know that soon I was to experience one of the most terrifying psychotic episodes of my life.

I know that there are parts of this that I don't entirely remember. But I do remember the arguments in the car. Peter was going on this trip against his will. It wasn't a fun family holiday. It was something to placate me and silence my demands. As we drove up to Holyhead, I became nastier and more threatening.

'If you turn the car back around,' I hissed at Peter, 'I will slam the handbrake on.' There were kids in the car, but that didn't mean anything to me. I was seriously ill. And no one took Peter seriously enough to do anything about it, so he had no choice but to keep going.

At other points I felt on cloud nine. I was going to Ireland! I was going to live my dream and finally go to the country that I longed to visit. I told Peter that I had no plans to return. He was frightened. This wasn't the woman he married. But he had to stay with me. People can't just get up one day and leave their entire lives without any money. He had to protect me.

On reflection now, I just wish someone had listened to Peter and believed that I was far more ill than they realised. I wish people had dealt with me properly. Not by just plonking me in a mental hospital and leaving me there, but by showing me some tender care, which I clearly so desperately needed.

We carried on arguing as the journey continued. Eventually we reached the ferry port. As things became more heated I told Peter that if he didn't want to come with me, he could go and I'd take the kids. I got out of the car and went to pay for the tickets.

When I got back to the car, Peter and the children had disappeared. I started to panic. Where the hell had they gone?

He must have driven onto the ferry in the car, I thought. *He'll come back to find me when he's finished.* I sat down and waited to be called to board the ferry. It was very late at night and I seemed to be waiting forever. I called Dad.

'I'm so excited, Dad!' I called down the phone. 'I'm finally off to Ireland!'

'Karen, this is ridiculous,' my dad said down the phone in a weak voice. 'You're going to turn your kids demented soon if you carry on this way!'

His words hit me like a slap in the face. Harm my children? I didn't want to do that. All I wanted to do was visit Ireland. Why would he say such a mean thing to me? I hung up the phone, upset. Still it didn't occur to me that I was mentally ill.

I continued to wait, starting to feel a bit nervous on my own. But I knew to stay where I was, otherwise Peter wouldn't know where to find me. I heard the announcement, calling me to board the ferry. Still I didn't question why I was alone. I just made my way onto the boat and found two lovely young gentlemen who seemed concerned that I was on my own.

They asked for a description of my car and tried to search for it for me. Clearly they thought that my situation and behaviour was odd and so they stayed by my side. They were obviously very worried for me and I feel so grateful to them now. I didn't know at the time how much danger I'd put myself in.

When we arrived at Ireland they just wanted me to be safe and reunited with my family, which sadly wasn't going to happen. They accompanied me to a gentleman who asked for my car's registration number, only to confirm my worst fear: neither my car nor my family had boarded the ferry. I felt sick and, for the first time, frightened. I was all alone in another country. Not only did I have no family or clothes with me, but I also had no money with me either.

One of the young men went and found someone who could help me. He seemed to take some convincing that this was a real situation. He didn't seem to have any sympathy with me as I was clearly uninjured. He couldn't see my mental illness. He told the garda to take me with them to the station, where they would get me the help that I needed.

I was terrified at this point. Being alone made me feel very vulnerable. I can vaguely recall answering lots of questions, and then I must have given them our home phone number. They tried to contact Peter, but after numerous failed attempts I began to fear that something had happened to them. After all, why wouldn't he answer? Surely they must have got back home a long time ago.

I was really worn out by this time. One of the guards told me to try and put my head down on the desk and get some sleep. It's funny the things that you can still recall while other details remain so elusive. I know, for instance, that I was wearing a long red cardigan. While I sat there, feeling hopeless, I found a little photo of Peter Anthony and Bernadette in my pocket.

I stroked the photograph and began to cry. Sobs racked through my body as I convinced myself that something dreadful had happened to my family. After some time the officer asked me if I had another number they could contact someone on. I don't know why I hadn't thought of that already, as Mam and Dad only lived around the corner, and so I gave them their number.

They managed to get through to Mam. She then went over to see Peter, only to find that on his return home he had unplugged the phone. The garda were furious. Who would leave their wife at a ferry port, unsafe, and out of her mind with worry?

Although I understand their anger, I understand now that it must have been an awful situation for Peter. It must have been extremely difficult to watch his wife going through all of this and not knowing what on earth was going on in her mind. To be fair, I didn't know what was going on, so how could anyone else? He also had his two young children to think of, and clearly he had to put them first. I was a danger to myself but I could have been a danger to my kids, and it was his job to protect them above all else. And Peter is only human, like everyone else. He was going through a lot of distress himself. I couldn't expect him to act perfectly in such harrowing circumstances. When a loved one goes through a mental breakdown, it is not just them that suffers.

The garda made plans to have me returned to Holyhead. In the meantime, they looked after me to the best of their ability. They sent out for fish and chips and made me eat some, encouraging me to stay strong and telling me that everything was going to be fine. They asked me why I wanted to be in Ireland and I just remember talking a lot about Daniel O'Donnell. They found it quite amusing, but in a very caring way. At one point I looked up and saw them watching the football. All I could make out was green Irish shirts. *Wow*, I thought to myself. *We're really not in the Boro, are we?*

That was the first moment I thought to myself: *Would I really want to leave my home town?*

Later that afternoon the garda told me that the ferry would take me back to Holyhead and Peter would be waiting there to collect me. They were very concerned that I would have to travel alone, but there wasn't really another option. I recall them giving me a ticket and telling me to get a drink and something to eat on the ferry. But I'd lost my appetite. I wanted to be back home and safe, but I was dreading the return journey.

At one point on the journey back I noticed an older lady who looked a lot like my nana Lizzie. For some strange reason I wondered if it could be her in another life. I longed to see a familiar face and so I projected the image of Lizzie onto her. It took a lot of self-restraint not to say anything to her. I'm amazed that I didn't.

I was bombarded with insane thoughts throughout the whole ride back, and it seemed to go on forever. I have never really felt so lost and so alone as on that trip. I was also seriously angry. I kept telling myself that when I saw our car I would smash it to bits. I was hurt and I felt ridiculed. I shouldn't have been left alone to make that journey all by myself and I was gearing myself up to punish my husband.

I disembarked and sat down on a bench, waiting again for Peter to appear. It was starting to get dark and I was cold and tired. No one arrived. Fury coursed through me. What the hell was going on? Was I being abandoned *again*?

I waited and waited, becoming more and more anxious. A member of staff passed by and I asked him for help. He didn't seem bothered; he just advised me to keep waiting. And so I did.

Eventually a pair of headlights came towards me in the enveloping darkness. Despite my anger I felt relieved that Peter had finally arrived. But it was short-lived. It wasn't our car driving towards us. It was a police car.

I was taken to a police station and asked a lot questions. By this point I was at the end of my tether. I'd simply I had enough. Somewhere, in a different room, Peter's voice rang out.

'I'm telling you, she's not right,' I heard him call. My blood began to boil.

For a lot of people with mental health issues, this is one of the worst things you can hear someone say about you. I immediately asked if I could be put into a cell.

'If you don't, I'm going to smash his face in,' I told them. They believed me and obliged.

A few hours later the police called an ambulance for me. Apparently I'd unnerved them enough to convince them I needed medical help. At last someone had realised how dangerous my illness really was. The issue, though, was that I was taken to a hospital that I had never been to before, and I had no idea where I was.

It turns out that the hospital was a mental health institution in Gwent, Wales, but I had no idea what was really going on around me. I continued to dip in and out of reality. I was utterly delirious and unsettled. I shouted, I screamed and I had hallucinations. I wandered out of my bed and refused to get back into it. I paraded up and down the corridors all night, feeling lost and confused. I kept trying to talk to the staff, but I don't think I was making any sense. My imagination ran wild and I pictured people who weren't there. I grasped at my head and shook it from side to side, trying to shake away my distress like a cobweb.

I didn't sleep that night, but I slowly managed to gain my composure. The following morning I met one of the other patients, who seemed like a nice girl. She kept me company and showed me where to go for breakfast. By now I had a bag of some my belongings with me that Peter had dropped off the previous night. But surely I wasn't expected to stay there for long?

It was a hot day. At some point we all sat outside together on the lawn as a group. Everyone was having a sing along and I could see a mountain nearby in the distance. It was beautiful. The scenery was just breath-taking. I lay down on the grass, my mind aching with confusion. I kept telling myself that I was going to pass away here. It didn't bother me like it should have done.

Sometime later one of the chaps from the group announced that he was going for a walk. I followed him and we ended up going to a nearby shop, where we bought ice creams. When I think about this now, I'm seriously shocked that I was allowed to do it. Why wasn't there anyone there to stop me, to tell me that walking off with a stranger while ill was unbelievably dangerous?

I clearly wasn't in a safe environment. I complained a lot and made a nuisance of myself. Maybe I just wanted them to kick me out, because all I wanted to do was leave and go back home. I needed to be safe with my family.

Thank God I was only there a few days. I was eventually told that they were going to discharge me and have someone escort me to the train station. My illness did not seem to bother anyone; they obviously felt this was the best decision. They'd apparently tried to have me transferred to our local hospital, but hadn't got anywhere with it.

Just before they discharged me, they gave me an envelope with my jewellery in it. As poorly as I was, I still knew that my engagement ring was missing. My gut instinct told me that a particular staff member knew something about it, and I asked her whether she knew where it was.

'It's not here,' she answered defiantly. 'It's not in the safe, so there's nothing I can do about it.'

'Well, then, I'll be involving the police,' I told her, with as much conviction as I could muster.

But it didn't seem to trouble her. She was taking advantage of a vulnerable person and she knew it. I knew I'd had my ring when I came in. I carried on arguing with her in the car to the train station, but it made no difference. She wouldn't budge.

When we arrived, I was given my belongings and a ticket for the train. I was then told to wait on the platform. They didn't wait for the train to arrive; they disappeared into the distance as soon as they could.

I got onto the train and felt sick to my stomach. I was anxious, tired, and angry. I looked out of the window and saw families waving goodbye to each other. I felt a pang of jealousy and I closed my eyes in exhaustion, leaning my head against the window.

The train began to move. I could hear other people talking around me. 'Yes, she's not well at all,' someone said nearby. I assumed this was about me. But I kept my eyes closed, trying to block out my paranoia. As the train went rushing through tunnels, the loud banging and the echo of the train assaulted my ears as though I was under attack. The chattering voices of the other passengers made me feel unsettled and frightened. I just wanted to scream.

As daylight appeared at the end of yet another tunnel, I opened my eyes and looked out of the window. I could see heaps and heaps of slag and I told myself that Middlesbrough had changed a great deal in the past few days. As the train came to a stop, I got off.

I looked around, hoping to see my children and my family. I looked out for Pepi, my Poodle, hoping he would be there waiting for me.

I looked at the town sign. I wasn't in Middlesbrough. I was in a town called Blaenau Ffestiniog in North Wales. But this didn't strike me as a cause for concern. I just sat on a bench, yet again, and waited to be collected. I looked out for a red car, as ours was red.

I thank God that nobody in a red car had pulled up or I would have just gone off with them. I waited and waited, certain in the knowledge that Peter would be there soon. Some time passed and eventually a sweet lady came and asked me if I was okay. I was kind of out of it at this point and just went with the flow of things. I explained my situation to her, and she took my hand in hers. She had a lovely, warm smile and I immediately felt safe with her. In a thick Welsh accent, she reassured me that she'd help me.

'Come with me, love,' she said to me, her brown eyes full of concern. 'I'll take you to someone who can help.' She took me to a local drop-in centre. There was a lovely middle-aged gentleman there who asked me lots of questions. I think he could tell that I was incredibly ill, even without my explanation of my time in hospital.

I don't know how he arranged it, but once again I was placed on a train and sent back to Llandudno, as this is where I had jumped on the wrong train. Someone somewhere decided that I should be taken back to the hospital, but there was a disagreement between them and the local police. The hospital refused to let me back in. I was only just able to follow what was going on at this stage. I could barely think straight or keep my head up and so most of these memories are a blur. All I remember quite vividly is being put onto yet another train next to a guard, who was tasked with keeping me safe. My poor brain was so frazzled. I wanted the train doors to be opened so that I could fling myself off it and end my torment. I'd had enough. I was alone in the world and no one understood how I was feeling.

When we arrived at Manchester I began to sob. The guard looked surprised; she had no idea what to say to me. But I didn't care any more. I had no more energy left. I was physically and mentally drained. My heart felt broken and I wasn't sure I had the stamina to get on a final train back to Middlesbrough.

I told myself that this was the final leg of the journey that would take me back to my family. I embarked alone. But obviously it had been proven by now that that was a bad idea. I followed a young couple and got off at Dewsbury. In my desperation I had considered them to be friendly people, based solely on how they looked. Thank God they were, because they agreed to help me after I approached them. They did for me what no one else had been willing to do: stay with me and make sure I didn't leave their sight. They called the police who looked after me and contacted Peter.

Finally, after so many twists and turns in my horrific journey, Peter came to collect me from the station. He told me he'd been waiting for me at Middlesbrough train station, and the family had become frantic with worry when I hadn't turned up. I didn't really respond to this; I didn't point out that he didn't seem too worried when he'd left me in Ireland. Instead I just climbed into the car and slept all the way home.

CHAPTER 16
A Return

Unsurprisingly, my story of my trip to Ireland shocked people. Some people were quick to try to lay the blame with Peter.

But I tried my best not to let it happen. Things had been strained and desperate and dangerous, and he'd had children to protect. He didn't know what condition I had. Hell, I didn't even know. The saddest part was that if people had bothered to listen to Peter in the first place, particularly my doctor, none of this would ever have happened.

In all honesty what I should have expected was the mental health hospital to take some responsibility for my wellbeing and at least ensure my safe return. Peter and Mam had been under the impression that I was to be transferred to another hospital near Middlesbrough, but it didn't happen. I also told Mam about my stolen engagement ring.

I knew she wouldn't let it pass. She always had my back. She called them and gave them some real grief, telling them that she refused to let them get away with theft.

How strange when the ring arrived in the post only a few days later!

But being back home couldn't suddenly make me well again. I was still incredibly poorly. At first I tried my best to carry on as normal and make things okay, but it wasn't long before I voluntarily admitted myself to the hospital. They sectioned me under the Mental Health Act and I was placed onto a ward with some other mentally ill patients.

It had to happen. I was seriously unwell. I'd quickly become convinced that I was the reincarnation of Jesus. I did my best to persuade everyone around me of the fact. I could recall, vividly, St Veronica wiping the tears off my face as I was led to the cross. I could remember the ridicule and jeering that I suffered before I was crucified. It hurt me deeply and left me feeling traumatised. Perhaps it was the humiliation of being ridiculed in real life that led me to feel this way.

The nurses in the hospital were subjected to my ramblings too. I was Jesus reincarnated, damn it, why wouldn't anyone believe me? They should have handled me far more sensitively than they did. I recall one nurse taking my hand and examining it closely.

'I can't find the stigmata,' she said to me, her voice dripping with sarcasm. 'Funny that, isn't it?'

It was very hurtful and totally unnecessary, but unfortunately it wasn't unusual behaviour from the staff in that hospital.

I couldn't even leave of my own will now because I'd been sectioned, and I'd lost sight of how poorly I was again. I pined for my children. I wanted to be with them all the time, but it wasn't safe any more. My heart ached for them, but I know now in hindsight that the separation was the best thing for me and for them. I had to become well again in order to function properly.

I was heavily sedated when things got bad. I stayed in bed, conked out, for a very long time. When I did finally come around, there was nobody around to take care of me. I tried to walk around and stumbled about, falling in the corridor. Apparently the level of care you received in that hospital was dependent on what time it was and how well-staffed the shift was.

I didn't really receive any counselling while I was in there. I was given medication but I was never diagnosed with anything other than anxiety and depression. Looking back, I wonder how, with all the insane things that I'd said and done, I wasn't assessed further. This was obviously more than just anxiety and depression. But it didn't occur to anyone, least of all me, to put another label to my condition.

I stayed in hospital for almost six weeks. Peter and Mam brought Peter Anthony and Bernadette to see me as often as they could. I tried to make the most of my time with them. I became bored very quickly. I listened to music a lot to distract myself when I felt well enough to do so. Thankfully, I can look back and smile when I hear those tunes now as there were some happier times during my stay, but that was more down to some of the nice staff and the patients that I met. My mind was still troubled and disturbed but slowly, little by little, I started to improve again. I was beginning to pull myself out of the mire.

Despite being in hospital I was always careful to look after myself and take great pride in my appearance. I've always placed a great deal of value on this, but even more so back then, as a young girl in my late twenties. Every morning I would wash my long, dark, curly hair and then go to the office. I would pull funny faces behind the backs of some of the nurses while I waited in line for the hairdryer. It always made the sister in charge, who was called Arlene, chuckle under her breath. The hairdryer stayed with the staff for safety reasons, but it gave me a real confidence boost knowing that they trusted me enough to even borrow the hairdryer. They even let me run over to the staff canteen in a morning to do a sausage butty run. Perhaps I wasn't a lost cause after all.

Some of the other patients also struggled to believe that I was a patient too. Many a time, when a new person came into hospital, they would often ask if I could be the nurse that looked after them. I'm convinced this is because I cared so much about the other people on the ward and tried my hardest to make them happy. Looking back now, I realise that this was a sign that I was getting better and pulling myself out of my psychosis. At my worst, I never gave a second's thought to other people's feelings; I was too busy being completely wrapped up inside my own mind.

I liked to help one of the older ladies, who was partially sighted, head over to the chapel on a Sunday morning. I would also get a dish of warm water to bathe her feet in. One morning I arranged for us all to do a fitness session to a video that I had. That must have looked hilarious: a bunch of mental health patients, all of various ages, on a ward doing exercises together. I also had us all watch films together, and persuaded Arlene to bring us chocolates to eat.

Whenever my friends visited, Sister Mary Frances would tell them that I was a breath of fresh air in the hospital, and it made me feel very proud. I'd hated feeling like a burden recently. Knowing that I was bringing some positivity to someone's life for a change helped me get through the weeks.

I had one very surprising repeat visitor: Uncle Barry. I had never really expected him to understand my plight. But I was wrong: he was so lovely and caring. He would sit with me and have a cup of tea, talking about anything I wanted to discuss. He always brought me some chocolates and tried to cheer me up if the depression got particularly bad.

He confessed that he wasn't happy with my dad. 'He doesn't try hard enough to understand what you're going through,' he admitted to me earnestly. 'It gets to me. You're his daughter. He should put in the effort. I try to tell him, but it doesn't really get through to him.'

I deeply appreciated him trying to talk to Dad, as it meant I finally had someone on my side who wanted to understand my mental illness. As much as he could, anyway, when none of us truly knew what I was suffering with. I'll never know how he came to be so knowledgeable about mental health, but it was very reassuring.

When the time came for me to leave, I found it hard to transition back into normal life. I struggled to get used to being at home and my new medication just completely knocked me out. I was sleepy all the time. It took a Herculean effort every day to get out of bed. My legs felt like lead and I could never keep my eyes open. Everything I did was such an effort. Even the simple act of washing the pots was an exhausting ordeal.

Desperate for some help, I started receiving counselling from a community psychiatric nurse. She arranged for Bernadette to start a pre-school nursery to help me out. It helped a bit, but something was still wrong. I wasn't functioning properly and I knew I couldn't carry on this way. What kind of life was this, feeling constantly shattered? There was no quality of life at all!

At this point I was still attending outpatient appointments, and so I confided to my doctor that I was really struggling with everyday life and that I needed to stop my medication. I didn't know how long I could carry on feeling so exhausted.

He looked at me, concerned, but clearly not believing that my medication was the issue. 'There are some other avenues we could explore to help you get your energy back,' he said, in an attempt to keep me on the tablets.

I shook my head, feeling determined. 'No. I'm convinced the pills are making me this tired. It's robbing me of my life.' I looked at him squarely in the eyes, hoping I'd be able to show him how desperate I felt. 'Please, can I come off them for a little while? Just to see what happens.'

He hesitated some more, but I could tell I was getting through to him.

'I'm a mother of two kids. I need my strength.'

He still wouldn't accept that my problems were down to my medication, but eventually he agreed to let me stop taking my tablets for a while. And lo and behold, it worked. Slowly but surely, I started to feel human again, like I was back in the land of the living. I'd had no other option, but it was hard work trying to face life without the safety net of my medication. It was far too easy to just take to my bed and hide away under my duvet.

I tried to return to normal by helping my mam look after Dad whenever I could. And as time went on, I became a little stronger. Day by day I could feel the difference in myself. I even started to accompany Dad to his appointments again. For a while we even thought he was getting better, and that the worst was over. But I'm sure it doesn't take a big stretch of the imagination to guess that this wasn't actually the case.

CHAPTER 17

Dad's Steady Decline

As Peter and I sat in the hospital waiting room, we talked about poor Dad and all the pain and illness that he'd suffered from. He'd found another lump in his neck.

We hoped that if he was to have another operation, this would be the one that would put him on the road to recovery with no more setbacks.

Dad's attitude was changing, too. When we first discovered he had throat cancer, Dad had been adamant that he'd never have a voice box put in. But as time had moved on, he later told us, he'd started to discuss the subject with a mate of his who was suffering with the same illness. They'd both changed their minds on the subject.

'A voice box is better than a wooden box, eh?' he joked.

I couldn't bring myself to smile. I hated hearing those words, but I suppose I was just thankful that Dad would have been prepared to do whatever it took to stay alive.

Back in the waiting room, Peter and I sat together in silence. I didn't know what to say, to be honest. It felt like there was a lump in my own throat and misery sat between us in the air.

Dad reappeared suddenly and started heading towards the exit at top speed. Immediately Peter and I jumped to our feet and hurriedly followed him out.

'What's going to happen, Dad? Are you going to go into hospital for another operation?' I asked him, a little bit breathless and I fought to keep up with him.

Dad stared at the floor as he spoke. He sighed heavily. 'No. There's nothing I can do, Karen. I just have to let nature take its course.'

At first his words didn't hit home. I looked at Peter, confused, unsure of what my dad was saying. Or maybe I just didn't want to admit that I knew,

'What do you mean?' I questioned him again, panic rising in my chest. 'Surely something has to be done. What on earth do you mean?'

He repeated himself, and then there was no misunderstanding.

Oh, good God, I thought to myself. I wanted to throw all of my insides up.

As we climbed into the car, Dad asked us to take him to the club. 'I need a pint,' he said, as casual as anything.

I didn't respond straightaway. I felt numb as his words echoed in my mind.

'Why can't they just remove the lump like they did before?' Peter asked my dad. 'Why is this so different?'

But Dad didn't have an answer for him. He just stayed silent and repeated his request for me to take him to the pub. I tried hard not to look at him, for fear of bursting into tears. Once again everything felt like one huge mistake.

We arrived at the club and went and sat down while Dad walked off to the bar. He had insisted on buying us all a drink, like this was any other normal day. When he reappeared, he seemed eerily calm. But internally I was panicking and trying so hard not to show it. I didn't want to scare him.

This wasn't meant to happen. After all, the consultant had virtually promised that if Dad never lit another cigarette again, he could make him better. He guaranteed it. Dad had kept his side of the bargain, so what the hell was going on?

At some point, while I was lost in my own little world of panic and fear, Dad started talking to his mate, the one who had the same diagnosis. Apparently, things were not looking too good for him either.

'Let's have a bet on who's going to last the longest,' Dad joked, while I looked on, horrified.

I knew this was only a knee-jerk reaction from the shock, but it was too much for me to bear. I stood up and stalked off to the toilets. I just needed a moment to myself.

Now that I was faced with the prospect of losing him forever, I was beginning to realise that I needed him more than I'd let myself believe. Some part of me still worshipped him, just like little Karen did all those years ago.

Fair enough, he hadn't understood my illness and perhaps he hadn't been very supportive at my most desperate moments, but things had been hard for him. They'd been hard for all of us. That didn't mean that I could handle not having him around.

And what about Mam? Poor Mam! She didn't even know what had been said today yet. How was she going to cope with the news?

I found my seat next to Peter again and tried to compose myself. My poor husband looked drained and sad. 'Your dad's been having some frank words with me,' he whispered into my ear.

'What's he said?'

'He told me he isn't bothered about himself any more,' said Peter, keeping an eye on Dad so that he didn't overhear. 'But he's concerned about how all of this is going to affect you. He doesn't want you to get ill again.'

Tears sprung at my eyes. Poor Dad. What a brave man. Here he was, having just found out he was dying, telling my husband that all he cared about was me. Here was proof that he really did love me. How could I have ever thought that he didn't?

'Dad,' I said, swallowing hard. 'We have to go home and tell Mam.'

He shook his head. 'I can't handle doing that, Karen.'

I took a deep breath, feeling the pressure mount behind my eyes. I know he didn't want pity. I know he wanted to handle this 'like a man'.

'Listen, I'll go home and have a little talk with her before you get in,' I said to him. He just nodded at me. I kissed his forehead. 'Don't be far behind me, okay?'

I walked away quickly before he could see the tears streaming down my face. I thought I was going to burst from trying to hold them in.

Peter followed me into the car. For a few moments we just sat there in silence, processing our shock. How on earth were we going to break the news to Mam? How would we be strong enough?

As we walked into Mam's house, she instantly knew that something was wrong. I tried so hard not to show my fear, but I guess I failed miserably. I was frightened.

Mam looked just as distressed as we were; none of us had been prepared for this news. We had all just taken it for granted that they had made him better before, so of course they would be able to make him better again. We hadn't prepared for any other situation.

Peter went home to be with the kids and told me to stay with Mam. We couldn't just deliver the news and then leave her alone to wait for Dad to come back. But I couldn't just sit there waiting in silence, either. I needed answers.

And so I rang the consultant. I suppose I just wanted him to tell me that Dad had got it wrong and that he could be helped. I wanted to be able to tell Dad it was all a mistake.

But the call just clarified what we already knew. I felt brave enough to ask the consultant how long Dad had to live. I don't know why I needed to know, but I couldn't put the phone down without asking the question.

'It's difficult to tell,' said the consultant, sounding uncomfortable and, to his credit, dismayed.

'Please, just give me an idea,' I whispered. I tried to sigh the heaviness away from my chest. It didn't work.

'He probably doesn't have long. We're probably looking at months.'

The room swayed around me and I tried hard to ground myself. I felt close to collapse. I somehow summoned the energy to thank the consultant and rang off. I turned to Mam and wrapped my arms around her.

'Listen, Mam,' I soothed her in between her sobs and wails. 'Listen, I know it's hard, okay? I know it's hard, but we have to be strong for Dad. We have to make life as normal and comfortable for him as possible, okay? He needs us.'

She nodded, doing her best to pull herself together. I hoped I'd convinced her – I wasn't certain I could be strong myself. Hadn't I proved that I wasn't mentally healthy enough for this kind of stress?

That evening, as I lay in bed, I couldn't stop myself from crying. I knew I had to do my best to stay well now, for my dad's sake. But I wondered how on earth I'd manage it. Images of that horrific night came flashing back at me; I could see my dad's gaunt, sunken face staring at me when I closed my eyes. How would I handle it when my most insane thoughts and feelings about my dad became real? Would I able to keep my grip on reality?

You must be strong, I told myself, over and over again. *This isn't about you this time. Dad needs you to keep it together.*

I promised myself, for the sake of my children, my husband, and my parents, that I would save my tears for late at night, when I could let them go in the privacy of my own room. But during the day, life had to go on as normal.

Over the coming weeks, Dad continued to visit the hospital. Once again Mam struggled to cope with them, especially now that she knew he was never getting better. And so I took it upon myself to make sure that I always went with him.

It felt like our time. We became closer and closer. I felt quite privileged that he wanted me there, especially after our turbulent past and how little he'd seemed to care over the years. I was still trying to fight my own illness and so I snatched sleep whenever I could get it. I'd often make him laugh when he came around and realised I'd fallen asleep too. I cherished the fact that we could still have a laugh together.

One day in the infirmary, the weather was making us all uncomfortable. A nurse complained about the temperature and opened a window.

'Listen to us moan,' she said with a chuckle. 'We'll all be complaining that it's too cold soon, especially when we get the snow.'

I smiled at her politely and she left the room. Dad looked at me.

'I don't know, I don't think I will be here to see the snow.'

A pang of sadness hit me in my heart. But I just smiled at him. This was the first time that Dad had actually acknowledged that he believed what we'd all managed to keep from him: that he didn't have long left.

There was a brief silence. Then he spoke again.

'There's things in life I really should have done,' he said earnestly. 'But there's plenty more that I shouldn't.'

I squeezed his hand. He didn't have to elaborate.

'We all make mistakes, Dad,' I replied. 'And we'll go on making them. But we'll always love you. So, so much.' He squeezed my hand back and didn't say another word.

I was becoming close to my dad in a way I never had before. I now had the chance to talk to him about some things that he didn't understand. One morning he woke up and found me asleep next to him.

'Some nurse maid you are,' he said loudly and chuckled, waking me up.

I laughed, but then I seized my opportunity.

'I'm not sure how much of a maid I'd be anyway, considering I'm always so poorly myself.'

He nodded, a smile still playing on his lips.

'You know, Dad,' I began, 'just as you can't help having this dreadful illness, I can't help having my mental illness.'

Dad looked down at the floor. 'I know you can't,' he said. 'But to be honest, Karen, I've never really understood it. And I've never tried to understand it.'

'I didn't need you to know what the problem was. Even I still don't know, really. I just needed to know that you'd help me through it, even if it was an invisible illness inside my head.'

He stayed silent at this, but that was okay. I knew he was sorry. He just wasn't sure how to articulate it.

The days became weeks, and soon the weeks became months. Dad had a trachea fitted to enable him to breathe properly. I felt so sorry for him, as he would cough and have to cover the hole in his neck with a hanky. It made him feel so embarrassed. He didn't like me eating my tea around him because of it, but I honestly wasn't bothered. All that mattered to me was I could be with him and talk to him, so I ate with them and visited them as often as I could. Peter was brilliant; he helped alleviate as much stress as he could by helping out with the kids. I guess he didn't want a repeat of my last mental breakdown, as well.

Dad's tumour continued to grow, which meant he was unable to eat and drink. As a result, he had to have a tube fitted in his neck. It felt like another mini-heartbreak for me; Dad would never again be able to enjoy his food.

For some reason, it angered me that that I could see Dad's tumour and all the time it was growing. I hated looking at it, knowing it was taking away his quality of life and soon his life itself. Dad's single bed was brought into the living room, and Mam and I would sit on it with him, watching TV.

One evening, when one of the district nurses called round for Dad's visit, she discreetly beckoned me into the kitchen. She was obviously very aware of Dad's tumour and the increase in size.

'I just think that now is the time to inform you of what might happen,' she said to me in a grave tone of voice. Fine, I thought. It makes sense that I needed to hear the worst that could happen.

The worst, though, was more horrific than I could have imagined and it filled me with terror. She really freaked me out. Earlier that day she'd witnessed a patient's tumour, similar to my dad's, burst when they were out in the hospital ward. She likened the scene to something on the film *Psycho*.

I don't really know why she felt she needed to share this. I wondered if she'd actually crossed some kind of professional line. Perhaps she just wanted me to be aware, and that she had the best intentions, but all it served to do was frighten me.

After she left, I told myself I wouldn't tell Mam what the nurse had said, but she knew something had upset me. I didn't want to say anything, but I thought that maybe she had a right to know considering she was the one who was alone with Dad all night. Mam should really have been receiving some nursing support, but there wasn't any available.

And so often we would find ourselves just staring at Dad's neck whenever we were with him. That can't have been pleasant for Dad. It was stressful for us too, and so we confided in a lovely male nurse about what we'd been told.

He had a really nice manner about him, and he managed to calm us down by telling us that this was not a common way for things to progress. It was a highly unlikely occurrence, he told us.

Dad stopped being able to go to the club, which effectively wiped out his social life. People had been wondering for a while now anyway as to why we'd allowed him to keep on going. But he was a very proud, determined man and nothing we could have said would have stopped him. He had to make his own choice about when to stop.

Other than the odd trip to the hospital when he accidentally moved his breathing tube, things just became a waiting game. We knew Dad was coming to the end of the road, and we wanted to make his passing as lovely as possible for him. Ideally we wanted him to be laid in his bed at home, with his favourite singer, Perry Como, playing in the background. We wanted to hold his hands as he quietly slipped away. But none of us knew what would really happen. That lack of control had my mental health teetering on the edge, but I held on as hard as I could.

We were fast approaching Dad's 60th birthday, which was two weeks after Father's Day. I suggested to Dad that he might want to invite his friends over and have a party in the garden. Dad seemed really happy with this.

He looked at me and said, 'Do you know, Karen there was a time when I never thought that I was going to reach my birthday?'

It was so bittersweet. I was so pleased that he'd had the chance to enjoy once last birthday. As soul-destroying as it was for his friends and family, it was wonderful for him. And it bolstered my spirits.

During this time a very good friend of the family sadly passed away. Dad was adamant he was going to the funeral. We all went together and he insisted on going to the cemetery. Mam and I watched Dad quietly from a distance as he looked over the grave, paying his last respects. We asked each other what could be going through his mind, knowing that he didn't have long to live himself. We did our best not to cry.

Always the joker though, he stepped away from the grave and joined us a few feet away.

'A very poor turnout today,' he said to us, winking. 'But it won't be like this at mine. There will be standing room only.'

CHAPTER 18
The End Approaches

There were very few hospital appointments now. Dad was becoming very tired and very weak. One day, as we were leaving the infirmary, we both sat on the wall waiting for Peter to collect us. He sighed heavily.

'I'm just tired, Karen,' he said. 'I'm too tired to carry on with this. I'm ready to go.'

Where I managed to find the courage to have this conversation with Dad, I don't know. But somehow I did.

'Are you scared, Dad? Do you think Nana is waiting for you on the other side?'

He smiled lightly, a joyless smile. 'I'm not worried, love,' he said. 'I know Mam's going to be there. I just want the good Lord to take me, and even if he calls me today, I'll be ready. I just want to go.'

I nodded. There was no way I could stop the tears now.

Father's Day was just around the corner and I wanted it to be as happy a day as it could be. Mam and I went out and bought Dad new shirts. We asked him if, with our help, he would like to go to a club in Redcar. To our delight Dad loved the idea. It wasn't going to be easy, but we were all prepared to make it happen, even if it was just for a very short while.

In the morning, we gave Dad his cards and presents. He was determined to get himself ready in his own time and enjoy the day. Mam cooked the Sunday lunch and I sat in the kitchen with the kids, as I always did on a Sunday. I helped them to read and write while Dad was upstairs having a shave.

But when I went upstairs to check on him, I knew something was terribly wrong. Dad was sitting on the side of the bath and struggling to breathe. He had managed to pull out his breathing tube again. I rushed to the phone to call an ambulance.

While waiting, we tried our hardest to keep Dad calm. We gently led him downstairs to where his oxygen bottles were. Very soon the paramedics were on scene and attending to Dad. They asked him a lot of questions, which he could barely answer as he was struggling to breathe. They wanted to know why he was sat leaning to one side.

'Because he can't breathe!' I shouted. I was getting really frantic by this point, and I just wanted them to get his tube back in. They got him into the ambulance and I went with him while Mum minded the kids.

Everything was rushed and frantic in the ambulance. The paramedics tried their best to get Dad's tube back in, as by this point he wasn't breathing and oxygen was difficult to administer. But no matter how hard they tried, they couldn't manage it.

'I'm going to put the sirens on, love,' the driver yelled at me as he sped up. A jolt of panic hit me square in the chest.

'Try not to be too alarmed,' said the paramedic who was working on Dad. He'd seen the look on my face when I realised why we'd had to start speeding up.

But I felt sick. I knew now that it was a real emergency. Dad's life was at risk. I prayed and prayed that after all this time, he wouldn't be taken away from me like this.

Despite my protests about wanting to be with him, I was taken into another room when we made it to the hospital. I was in bits and couldn't stop crying. An eternity later the paramedic came to find me and assured me that they'd managed to get Dad's breathing tube back in. He was going to be okay.

I went to find him. He looked completely exhausted. I looked up at the nurse and asked her how long she thought Dad had to live. In hindsight I know I shouldn't have asked her. I guess she had no real way of knowing anyway.

Suddenly Dad interrupted our whispering. 'Doesn't look like we're getting to the club now, does it, Karen?' he said sadly. I said nothing.

A few days later it was suggested to us that we take Dad to a hospice. It wasn't ideal, but it would give us a chance to recharge our batteries. I knew it was vital for me to get home to sleep, as sleeplessness was clearly a trigger for my mental illness. Dad was transferred to the hospice, from the hospital, on the Tuesday.

Once again, Mam didn't really feel comfortable visiting him very often. She hated the idea of the hospice, and so Susan and I went along to settle Dad into his room. He didn't seem to mind being there. Perhaps it made him feel safe, as the calcium levels in his blood were making him confused. We didn't plan for him to be in there long, though. We still wanted to bring him home.

I took my son Peter to visit his granddad, and I was overjoyed when Dad asked where Bernadette was. I explained that he would be seeing her soon, but it made me happy that he remembered her despite his confusion. Perhaps we really would be able to bring him home.

The following day Mam and I went to see him. When we got there we found him sitting out in the corridor, looking alone and disoriented. Staff were just walking past him, showing him no attention or concern.

'Dad, are you okay?' I asked him, sitting next to him. It was then that I realised that his breathing tube had been dislodged yet again. He was struggling to breathe. Mam saw it too and rushed to find a nurse. She was quickly followed by a doctor and a group of more nurses, all of whom helped him back to his room and attempted to re-fit his tube. Mam and I were fuming.

'Why weren't they keeping a closer eye on him?' Mam yelled at the lady in charge. 'He's here for a reason, and you're not looking after him properly!'

I stood aside while she argued with them. I was too tired to get involved. And all it really got us were some more reassurances that the team would do all they could to help Dad get settled once again. It hardly made us feel better, but there was nothing else we could do. We went home, feeling uncomfortable and helpless.

That night I stayed with Mam, as we were both seriously upset and knew we wouldn't be able to sleep until we'd received a phone call. We needed to know that they'd managed to fit his breathing tube again and that he was out of danger. We rang the hospice a number of times, desperate for an update. It wasn't until very late in the evening when we were assured Dad was comfortable, although they'd still not managed to fit the tube back in.

We were beside ourselves. How on earth was Dad coping? We prayed that he was receiving oxygen and that it was keeping him alive. That night we lay in bed and talked, trying to get to sleep at times but failing miserably. It was a restless night that brought us no relief. I worried and worried that this would knock me back and affect my mental health.

At 8am Mam's phone rang and I answered it.

'Is that Karen?' asked a voice asked on the other end.

'Yes, it is,' I replied. 'Who's calling, please?'

The lady then introduced herself as a staff member from the hospice. 'I'm calling to tell you that your dad has fallen during the night. He was on the toilet.'

'Oh God,' I muttered, walking around the room and trying to find my clothes. 'I'll be there as quickly as I can. I just need to get dressed —'

'Karen,' the lady interrupted. 'I'm so sorry to tell you this, but sadly your dad has passed away.'

The floor was ripped from underneath me and the room started to spin around me.

'He's died?' I asked. Mam overheard me and started to wail.

'I'm so sorry,' said the lady on the phone.

'Can I come and see him?' I asked through choking sobs.

'Yes, of course you can.'

Poor Dad was laid out on his bed when I arrived. He looked as though he'd suffered a lot of pain, though maybe that was my mind projecting it onto him. Apparently he'd been on the toilet and had suffered a pulmonary embolism.

'Why didn't you wait for me?' I asked his lifeless body, anger and grief ripping through me. 'This isn't what we had planned, Dad. This isn't what we wanted for you. You should have been at home with us when it happened. Where you belong.'

We wanted answers. Had his breathing tube been put back in at any point in the night? How long had he been lying on the bathroom floor before somebody came to help him? Why had he been allowed to die on his own?

I felt incredibly guilty, that I'd let him down somehow. We had nursed him and looked after him for almost two years, and in just two days of being in the hospice he had been taken away from us. That wasn't right, surely?

Breaking the news to my children was one of the hardest things I'd ever done, even with all the crap I'd been through over the years. They were only two and four years old, but they understood why

I was crying and held me tightly. They'll never know how much of a comfort that was to me. It actually made me smile to hear them talking about how Dad had passed away. They'd overheard a bit of the story as we'd obviously accidentally spoken too loudly, but their interpretation of the events warmed my heart. Peter Anthony told Bernadette that their granddad had sat on the toilet, pulled the chain and gone straight to heaven. It made me chuckle, though I was quick to point out that didn't always happen when people went to the loo!

It is a very strange feeling that you have prior to a funeral. It feels like you're in limbo. You can't really get on with grieving. There's lots of people to see and speak to, and it's a seriously busy time. But perhaps that's actually what I needed. It was when I was allowed to wallow in misery that my mental illness would strike. While I had something to keep me occupied I felt grounded and rooted in reality. I had something to keep going for, a reason not to give up.

Dad wasn't a practising Catholic, but we knew that he would have wanted a full Catholic requiem mass. He didn't practically live in the Church like Nana had, but he'd always believed in God.

We met with the priest and gave him a little bit of background about Dad. I didn't mention the domestic violence. It wasn't appropriate in a funeral anyway, but something inside me felt that this was a good opportunity to let those demons go. I remembered how, in a previous psychotic episode, I'd screamed at him in anger about all the violence he'd inflicted on us. I didn't want to experience that again. And in his own way, he'd apologised for it. At that point in my life it was the closest thing to closure I could get on the subject. I wasn't receiving counselling and so I had to employ the classic Karen coping mechanism: tamp it down deep into the depths of my mind where I could pretend it had never happened.

There was no way we could have coped with a wake at Mam's house. Mam would still have to live there afterwards and it would have been far too traumatic. I preferred to go to the chapel of rest and pay my last respects to Dad in private there. We made plans to have a little celebration of Dad's life at the pub afterwards, with all of Dad's friends and family. And I thought it would be nice if, at the end of the service, we played a Perry Como song. I chose For *The Good Times*, which, to me, was very apt. That's what I wanted to remember about Dad. I had no more room in my fragile mind for bad memories.

Dad wasn't wrong about how many people would be at his funeral. There were crowds upon crowds of people there. I think I drew my strength from all of these people that day. I'd been convinced that I wouldn't be able to cope when the time came. But it's amazing how strong I felt. I found that if I reframed my thinking – seeing it as a day of celebration rather than mourning – then I could get myself through it. He would not have wanted me to spiral into a psychotic episode.

I was here for him. And this day was all about Dad.

There wasn't a dry eye in the church as the music played.

Don't look so sad, I know it's over, but life goes on, sang Perry Como. *And this old world will keep on turning.*

CHAPTER 19

The Nightmare Becomes a Dream

It was never going to be easy moving on without a dad in my life. But somehow, unlike all the times before, I remained strong for the sake of my beautiful children. I was twenty-nine now; it wasn't all about me any more.

For a little while they stayed with me at Mam's house. We didn't want her to feel as though we were just going to abandon her. Filling the house with the little ones' laughter helped. But we could only stay there a couple of weeks before getting our own lives back on track. I didn't want my poor mother getting too used to us being there, as it would be harder for her when we returned home. At least she still had Pepi, our poodle, to keep her company.

At some point Mam broached the idea of taking me back to Ireland. Surprisingly, despite the manner in which I'd visited last time, this really excited me. It was an opportunity to go and do it correctly this time. I wanted to lay old ghosts to rest.

It meant a lot to me to have the chance to go to Ireland in good mental health. Mam also felt that we both needed a break after everything we'd been through over the last two years. Dad had put a little money to one side for her and she'd decided to spend it on this. It was one last treat for us from Dad.

We had always wanted to go to Kincasslagh. It wasn't a coincidence that that was where Daniel O'Donnell was from. It also looked absolutely beautiful in the pictures. We arranged to go in the October when the festival was on, as there would be plenty for us to do. I booked our flights and arranged for us to stay in a little family run guest house.

We had to take a train to Scotland and then fly from there straight to Donegal. I was so excited. The difference between how I felt last time – when I'd completely lost the plot, feeling angry and aggressive – was huge. Now I was making the journey in a positive frame of mind, albeit still mourning my father. What made it even more special was that when we landed at the airport we were driven to Kincasslagh, with a group of others, by none other than Daniel's sister Kathleen. We were really chuffed!

Our first evening out was in the Viking Hotel, previously owned by Daniel. As we sat there having a couple of drinks, in walked Daniel O'Donnell himself. We couldn't help it; we both started giggling like teenagers at the thought of me coming here last time in pursuit of him. We needed a bit of light relief; I that was our way of dealing with the stress that my mental illness had caused the family.

It felt quite surreal to think that we were now sitting in the same bar as Daniel. While I was ill, I'd written a lot of letters to Daniel talking about my spiritual beliefs. He'd probably never even seen them, but I still felt a little embarrassed and wanted to explain that I had not been well. The letters must have been quite strange to read.

And so, when Daniel left the hotel, I took the plunge and hurried out after him. I tapped him on the shoulder and he turned around. He smiled at me. 'Can I help you?'

I blushed but held my nerve. 'Daniel, I'm a huge fan. Would you do me the honour of having a little walk along the shore with me while I'm here on holiday?'

He looked very taken aback and shook his head apologetically. 'What would I do if a thousand and one people wanted to walk along the shore with me?'

I felt my face go red with embarrassment.

'But don't let that stop you from walking along the shore. That area really is lovely.' He walked away.

I'm not sure what I'd been expecting, but somehow I still felt stunned at his response. I felt annoyed with myself, as he had probably thought I was some crazy fan, which really wasn't the case. He didn't even have any idea that I was the one who'd written all those strange letters to him! That is, if he'd ever even received them. I had just always felt we both had a very strong faith and wanted to communicate that to him. But of course he couldn't have just gone swanning off with anyone just because they told him they were a fan. I hurried back into the hotel and told Mam we were leaving.

As we walked back hurriedly to the guest house, I explained to Mam what had been said. I must admit I had a few choice words to describe Daniel, and none of them were very tasteful. I felt angry and bitter that I hadn't had the chance to explain away the actions brought on by my mental illness. I wanted Daniel to know that it wasn't what defined me, and that I was actually a completely different person when I was mentally well. And I hadn't had that opportunity. Why did I still care so much, after all these years, what people thought of me? Even now it was still navigating so much of what I did in my life. I was frustrated with Daniel but I was also really quite frustrated with myself.

We continued along the very dark road, with me still babbling on, when all of a sudden I spun round to see a very large truck approaching.

'Oh my God!' I shouted, as I tried to find somewhere we could go in order to get out the way. But there were no paths, and so I just shoved Mam to safety on a nearby grass verge. It took me a few moments to realise that I'd actually pushed us both into a ditch.

I managed to climb out, which was not an easy task in high heels, and then attempted to help Mam out. But it was to no avail. The headlights from the truck were getting closer and closer, and so I frantically waved my arms to get the driver to stop. The next thing I knew, two burly drivers had climbed out to assist me in our hour of need. They helped Mam out of the ditch and ensured we were both fine before driving off.

Well, at this stage Mam and I were just howling with laughter and couldn't stop. It had been just like a scene from a *Carry On* film. And thank God it had happened – it had stopped my downward spiral and got rid of my negative thoughts.

The next morning Mam was attempting to get out of bed and realised that she couldn't put her foot down. She'd obviously done something to her ankle in the fall. Maybe it was because she'd had so many drinks that she hadn't really felt it last night. Still chuckling, we got a taxi to Dunloe hospital and a couple of hours later Mam emerged with crutches. She'd badly sprained her ankle. Thankfully, she has a brilliant sense of humour and was determined to continue to enjoy the holiday.

That evening we were going to see Daniel in a little concert in the marquee at the rear of his hotel. I had a right face on me, but I pretended to be joking as I told her that I wasn't sure I wanted to see him now. I still felt a little bit embarrassed. I soon learnt I'd have to suck it up, though, as Mam was given a disabled seat in the front row. *Typical*, I thought. Now we'll be the first pair of faces he sees as he steps onto the stage. It's really quite funny now, in hindsight.

We had a great time on the holiday, but I still couldn't get that first evening out of my mind. I still really wanted to let Daniel know the reason that I'd wanted to go walking with him. I decided there was nothing more for it: I was going to have to write yet another letter of explanation.

At the end of the church service that Sunday, I noticed that Daniel was there in the congregation. This was a good opportunity to give him my letter. I'd been fretting about it for days. I didn't want him to get the wrong impression of me, but this needed to be done.

Somehow, I summoned the courage to walk over to him and hand him the letter. I even managed to ask him to promise me he'd read it. To give the man credit, he promised he would. Breathing a sigh of relief, I walked away and joined my mam, who was lighting a candle and saying a prayer. I allowed myself to relax and closed my eyes in prayer.

I didn't stay relaxed for long, though. As I opened my eyes I spotted Daniel. He'd already started reading the letter. A jolt of nervousness and anxiety kicked in and I hurried Mam along. I couldn't face being there when he read about some of the most personal words I'd ever written in my life.

That evening we attended a ball that took place every year. As part of the tradition, Daniel always had a different belle, usually a celebrity, to accompany him. He would sit blindfolded until his belle was revealed. This year he was in for a real treat, as his belle was none other than Loretta Lynne.

Loretta is a huge country star and everyone knew that Daniel idolised her. At one point in the evening Daniel asked if we would all like to come forward and meet Loretta, so we all formed an orderly queue. Just as we were nearing the front and shaking hands with Loretta, Daniel caught my eye and pulled me to one side. Butterflies fluttered about in my stomach.

'I've read your letter, Karen,' he told me warmly, squeezing my arm in a comforting gesture. 'Please forgive me for not being very understanding. And thank you for being so open and honest – it must have taken a lot of guts to do that.'

A wave of relief washed over me. What a gentleman. He was just as lovely as I'd always imagined him to be. I know some people may find this difficult to understand, but it meant so much to me. It felt like now I'd managed to strengthen a link between me and Dad, somehow. It was his music that we had both shared a passion for; we had this mutual admiration for Daniel. And now, knowing that both Dad and Daniel accepted my mental illness, I could be at some kind of peace with the past and with myself. It was okay not to be okay all of the time.

Not long before we lost Dad, Peter and I went to a Daniel O'Donnell concert in Bridlington. At the end, I was determined to meet Daniel and ask him if he would kindly ring Dad to wish him all the best with his treatment. He was lovely and agreed to do it. A few weeks later I went into Redcar to do some shopping and when I got home my dad called round. I was absolutely delighted when he told me that Daniel had called him. He acted so cool about it, but I knew that it meant so much to him. He bragged about it to his mates and it put a huge smile on his face. This is how wonderful a man Daniel O'Donnell is.

That week away in Kincasslagh was just the tonic that Mam and I needed. When Daniel likens it to heaven, I understand completely what he means. I went on plenty of long walks alone, which cleared my mind and helped me to relax. There's a unique kind of silence that falls over you when you walk across the Frosses. I would never forget this special place, especially after experiencing it in far more positive circumstances.

At last I had visited my beautiful Ireland.

CHAPTER 20

We Spiral Once Again

That break with Mam was just what the doctor ordered. We returned armed with gifts for everyone and a determination to pick up the pieces of our lives. We knew Dad would have wanted us to move on, but that's far easier said than done. Our first Christmas without him was hard. It felt hollow and incomplete, like the pages of a favourite book had been ripped out.

The following year Peter managed to find little bits of work. Being a pipefitter meant that he was often unemployed and as a result he had to take what he could get. For this reason he had to go away to work for a few weeks at a time. At some point he was offered work which required him to be away for the whole week, and he would only return on weekends. We had no choice. Financially, things were unstable due to my erratic spending habits in the past. We didn't envisage this for our lives, but Peter had no choice but to give it a try.

My 30th birthday was looming on the horizon. I should have been happy and excited, but I felt kind of numb. Everything seemed a bit grey and lifeless. It was at this point that I knew something was wrong.

I was terrified that I was becoming poorly again. And the worst part was that I had no idea how to react to the warning signs. The grief of losing my dad and worrying about our financial issues was causing me to lose sleep. And I knew what that had done to me in the past.

I also couldn't concentrate on anything. I would try to watch TV and find that at the end of the programme I'd barely taken anything in. I often felt that the people who I'd lost of the years were around me, guiding me. Sometimes this was a nice feeling, but at others it made me feel a bit invaded and unsettled. Peter had disappointed me as he'd called to tell me he wouldn't be home for my birthday party, and I couldn't shake off that feeling of being a bit betrayed. He knew it was going to be hard anyway without my dad there.

What's more, I started to lose a lot of weight. I became utterly obsessed with working out. Often it was all I could think about. Combined with my lack of sleep, it was making me feel ill and lethargic.

I celebrated my 30th with Mam and the kids. It was nice enough, but it felt lacklustre and unsatisfying. I knew then that it was more than just disappointment: I was struggling to find the joy in anything at all.

The day after my birthday, I planned to go to the church and then visit Uncle Barry. I set off, taking Peter Anthony and Bernadette to school on the way. As I went into nursery with Bernadette, she became agitated and screamed that she didn't want to go in.

'It'll be okay,' I tried to reassure her, knowing that in my current state I couldn't handle any hassle today. My mind was fragile and unsettled, and any kind of stress would throw me off course.

'Nooooo!' Bernadette screamed, wriggling out of my arms and away from the entrance. I sighed heavily.

'If you come in, Bernadette, we can do some painting today,' the teacher coaxed her, kneeling down and smiling. But it didn't work. She utterly refused to budge, and so I had no choice but to take her with me. She clearly wasn't feeling great.

And so it was that I had Bernadette with me when I approached Uncle Barry's house. I didn't normally like to do this, as Uncle Barry wasn't great at keeping his house in order. But nevertheless I knocked at the door.

There was no answer. A cold feeling crept over my shoulders. Something was horribly wrong.

I walked around the edge of the house, trying to look into the windows. I couldn't see Uncle Barry, but that didn't matter. I could smell death.

Knowing that Uncle Barry was lying somewhere in the house, I started to panic. My breathing became laboured. I didn't have a spare key, and so I couldn't get in. I walked away and down the road with Bernadette in tow. I felt like a funeral director leading a procession. For a split second, I was convinced that that's what I was.

I snapped myself out of it almost immediately. *What on earth is the matter with me?* I thought to myself. I tried to keep calm as to not alarm Bernadette, but inside I was freaking out.

When I got home I told Mam what had happened.

'He's dead in there,' I said, shaking and weepy.

'Karen, it's fine,' said Mam. 'Just 'cause he's not home, it doesn't mean anything's wrong. He's probably down at the club like he always is. Give him a ring.'

But I could smell his body, I thought as I dialled the number of the local club. I knew they would tell me he wasn't there.

'Yeah, hang on love, I'll just go and get him,' the barman said into the phone. I blinked rapidly during the ensuing silence.

'Karen?' My uncle's voice found me through the receiver.

'Barry, you're okay.' I exhaled heavily.

'Karen, love, I'm sorry I missed your birthday. I completely forgot. I feel really bad.'

'It's fine, it's fine,' I said, shaking my head. I expected the anxiety to melt away, but it didn't. Instead I told him about what I'd been worrying about. I knew, from previous conversations, that he'd understand – no matter how crazy I sounded.

He told me that he understood, and would call to see me later in the day. He reassured me that he'd drop off a spare key as well, so that I could feel more relaxed. I thanked him and hung up, but I didn't relax. I couldn't shake off that feeling of impending death. It scared the hell out of me.

Peter came home a few days after this. He took one look at me and started to worry.

'You're getting poorly again,' he said to me. 'How much weight have you lost? Have you been sleeping?'

Of course I hadn't. I was already on the slippery slope and I had no way of stopping it.

My CPN came to visit and she expressed the same worries as Peter. She knew all about my past and did her best to intervene.

'Karen, would you be willing to go back into hospital as a voluntary patient?' she asked me.

I shook my head at first, determined not to be beaten yet again. 'I have to look after the kids.'

'I'm sure your family will help you out,' the nurse replied. 'It's best to go in now, before things get really bad again.'

I hated the idea. I was annoyed with myself for discussing my disturbed thoughts with her. But I could see the warning signs as well as she could, and as much as I wanted to avoid the hospital, I wanted to avoid a breakdown even more. And so it was that I was sectioned again and placed onto a ward.

The next week in there was hard. I cried all the time. Strange thoughts punctuated my normal ones. Sleep was elusive. I thought obsessively about my weight and couldn't get that stench of death out of my mind.

And then one day Peter and Mam visited me, both of them looking distressed.

'Oh, Karen,' Mam said, tears in her eyes. 'Uncle Barry was found collapsed in his house the other day. He's very poorly.'

Blood rushed about in my ears. What?

Mam continued to explain. Nobody really knew what had happened to Uncle Barry yet, but they assumed it had been connected with his alcohol intake. I demanded to be taken to see him, as something in me knew that time was against us. I wanted to say my goodbyes.

But this was a task in and of itself, as I was sectioned now. I had to go to great lengths to be let out. I couldn't convince anyone that I'd had a premonition, that my thoughts were far from coincidental. It just didn't ring true to those around me, and I can see why.

Eventually I was allowed to leave the hospital with Mam and Peter, as long as I returned soon after my visit. I wasn't prepared for what I was about to see. My poor uncle was close to death. There was a terrible smell in the room, as his body was just giving up on him.

I started thinking about the last few times we'd interacted with each other. When Dad passed away, Uncle Barry had come to see me and asked if I would be a beneficiary of his will. He wanted to leave his money to me, as long as I promised him that I would make sure he was buried next to his late brother. I didn't think anything of it at the time – he was only 59 – and so I just figured that he was being sensible. I wondered now whether he knew, much like I had seemed to know outside his house, that the end was near. I felt saddened, sickened and creeped out.

The following morning, back in hospital, I was woken by one of the nursing staff. They told me that Barry had passed away.

I sat in my bed, crying into my mug of tea. How much more of this could I take? How much more of my family was I going to lose? And how much of my sanity would be left when all of this finished?

How had I known something was going to happen to him, just like I'd foreseen my dad getting ill? Was it pure coincidence, or did I have some kind of strange ability to predict the future? Was it even 'normal', or 'sane', to think that I might be having premonitions? What was happening to my mind when this stuff happened? If it was just all coincidence, why couldn't I just see it that way?

Clearly it wasn't just simple anxiety or depression. I'd never read anything about these symptoms in relation to depression.

Despite being sectioned, I needed to arrange some leave to organise another funeral. I also had to empty my uncle's property, as it was my job to do it. Peter and I arranged to meet a friend of my uncle's and get started on the house. Uncle Barry had asked me in his will if I would arrange for one of his friends to have his air gun, and for another to get his expensive binoculars. And so this is what I did.

I then set about emptying the house. To be honest it was difficult to know where to begin. There was so much to be done. It was decided that the old-fashioned furniture would go to auction and any junk I would just have removed. We all pitched in and helped.

I also helped to arrange the funeral. I organised a little celebration of Barry's life in the local pub. He was even buried just behind Dad's grave. I should have been pleased that I'd managed to sort things to Barry's liking, but in all honesty I was just going through the motions. I'd descended back into whatever kind of madness that I seemed destined to suffer from forever, and now instead of grief I just felt shocked and numb. I felt powerless to do anything about it.

But being out of the hospital had given me a little sense of freedom again. When Peter and Mam told me I had to go back to the hospital (as technically I was still sectioned) I became incredibly agitated and angry.

'I just want to be at home with my kids!' I yelled at them both. 'And why shouldn't I be? I'm an adult. It's my choice!'

Mam and Peter felt the full force of my fury as I fought them all the way, right up until the day I had to go back. But it was inevitable that I had to return, as this kind of behaviour felt all too familiar. Peter was experiencing a repeat of that horrible experience back in Ireland. He was, once again, at the receiving end of my extreme aggression and I didn't want things to end badly again. And so I bit the bullet and went back.

CHAPTER 21
A Betrayal and a Breakdown

It was 1999, and I was to spend a few more weeks in hospital, where my psychotic episode thankfully died down. I was just thankful that it hadn't resulted in as much erratic or bizarre behaviour as before.

After all that I'd been through, I was desperately hoping that I could get through a year of good health and happiness. Perhaps it was for this reason that I went into into the year feeling optimistic. I guess that's what made Peter's betrayal all the more hurtful.

A few months into the year, Peter confessed to me that he'd had a one-night stand while working away. I was absolutely devastated. I didn't care if it had lasted one night or ten years. To me, Peter had had an affair. And that wasn't acceptable.

I reacted as I'd always assumed I would react if faced with this kind of situation: I told Peter to leave. For me, there was no going back.

He didn't put up a fight. He moved out of the house. Unfortunately, he could only find accommodation in a hostel, and although part of me felt guilty about that at the time, it wasn't enough for me to ask him to come back.

'If you'd stayed in the house with me, I'd have only made your life hell,' I hissed at him, my insides twisted with pain and anger. I let my fury eat me up inside and I didn't handle our break-up appropriately.

I lashed out at him and failed to hide it from my kids. I destroyed all of our photos and anything in the house that reminded me of him.

Looking back now, of course I wish I had handled this with more dignity. But I'd only just recovered from another mental breakdown. This was a knee-jerk reaction and at that time I felt that I was entitled to it.

Eventually the council gave him another house to live in. I thought that maybe that would solve things. I didn't have to feel bad about him being in a hostel. And for a while it worked, but then he was burgled.

I know, I know, it was no real reason to get back together with him. But I felt sorry for him, and I think I mistook that for forgiveness. Somehow Peter managed to convince me to let him come back to our house and give things another go.

But it didn't work out. Of course it didn't. I'd lost all trust in him, and I didn't respect him any more. I felt nervous and paranoid every time he left the house. I was constantly in tears and my heart ached. It was a huge blow to my self-esteem and I wondered how he could bring himself to be with another woman when he apparently loved me so much. What had gone wrong? Did it say anything about me? Was I not attractive any more? Was living with me and my mental illness too stressful? Or was I putting too much blame on myself?

It just became too much. I couldn't handle the heartache any more. I'd been sending out very mixed signals, I know, but at least I could say I'd given it a shot.

I was terrified of asking him to leave again. I didn't want him to react badly. But deep down I think both of us knew that there was no way forward. I hired a solicitor and started divorce proceedings.

As I packed up his belongings while Peter was at work, the anger and resentment ate me up inside. I raged about, furious at the audacity of what he'd done to me. I couldn't hide my tears from my kids or my mother.

It didn't take me long to spiral into yet another bout of depression and psychosis.

I didn't want him to notice I'd become ill again. I didn't want him and Mam to think that this was a sign that the break-up shouldn't happen. I'd made my decision and I was going to stick with it, even if it had made me ill. I took the power out of their hands, called the doctor, and begged him to admit me to the hospital.

I knew I didn't need to be sectioned this time, as my symptoms were mild compared to how bad they'd been before. But I needed a break from reality. As such, the doctor just acted as though I was wasting his time. He huffed about and sighed a lot, making me feel like nothing but trouble. I felt embarrassed but I stood my ground, and eventually he rang a taxi. He let the hospital know that I was on my way.

I cried so much when I arrived. I felt so alone but too scared to tell my family where I was. I stayed overnight, of course without a sleeping for a second.

The next morning the doctor visited me on his ward rounds.

'Karen, you'll be staying here for a little while,' he told me, nonchalantly. 'I'm afraid to say that you've been sectioned again.'

'What?' Why had I been sectioned? They were aware that I just needed a break, that's all! I wasn't crazy enough to be sectioned again! I was furious. I'd voluntarily walked through that door!

The irony was the doctor who hadn't wanted to admit me was the one who'd eventually signed my section form. I couldn't believe it. What's more, the social worker who'd seconded the section told me that, as it was most unlike me to *want* to be in the hospital, they were convinced I'd attempt to leave before I was well.

I just couldn't win. Surely I should have been praised for finally having some insight into my illness? I was seriously frustrated. I had begged for help and now I was being treated as though I couldn't be responsible for myself.

I argued continuously with the staff, but they had no intention of listening to me. Every time I spoke, it seemed to undermine my credibility.

I made a big mistake when I mentioned my divorce. To my absolute astonishment, when I told them about what had happened with Peter, they got in contact with the solicitor, telling her that I wasn't in the right frame of mind to make such a big life decision. It beggared belief.

'Listen to me,' I said to the solicitor down the phone. 'I know full well what I'm doing. My husband cheated on me. I'm not interested in staying married to him. I don't care how mentally ill I am; I know I'm making the right decision!'

'Karen, it's okay,' she reassured me. 'I know that when we met and talked about this, you were well. I understand how you're feeling. I won't stop the divorce proceedings if you don't want me to.'

Well, that was something at least. But the hospital staff continued to question everything I ever mentioned about my private life. It was as though they were desperate for confirmation that I didn't know what was going on around me. But I did. I wasn't completely lost just yet.

It seems such a shame, especially now, that they didn't put as much effort into making me well and investigating why I was becoming ill all the time. All of these years later and I still had no answer. I didn't know what was wrong with me, but what was worse was that the staff didn't know and they had no intention of finding out, either. I seemed destined for a life of misery interspersed with fleeting moments of wellness. It was no way to live and I was growing tired.

Yet again I was released with no real solution to my ongoing problems. I just had to ride out my psychosis and depression and wait for it to pass. When it did, I was sent back home with no more answers than I had when I'd gone in.

On my return home, Mam stayed over to look after me and Peter stayed at hers. I was adamant that the divorce was still going ahead, and I had no intention of living with Peter as a couple. It is easy to look at things very differently in the heat of the moment, but I still believe I made the right choice. We'd both been through an awful lot in such a short time, but that was no excuse really.

At this point my bouts of illness became more and more frequent. I had no support – I wasn't getting any kind of counselling any more, and no more medication either. And as a result, that irrational, carefree, risk-taking Karen crawled her way up to the surface again. I felt indestructible and began my own affair.

I know it wasn't the answer, but somehow it felt satisfying to get my own back. Rightly or wrongly, I'd always told Peter that if he ever let me down I would do the same to him. Because of this, my affair was doomed to failure. I didn't care at the time, though, even when it all ended in tears. And all it served to achieve was to convince Peter that our marriage really was well and truly over.

It was during this time that another horrible coincidence befell my life. My Uncle Des was diagnosed with the same illness that Dad had had: throat cancer. What's more, he was 59 years old – the exact same age that Dad and Uncle Barry had been when they died.

By now it was the year 2000 and every loss I'd experienced had been like a full body blow. This next one wasn't as devastating as losing my dad, but it was particularly distressing because I was so depressed. It also terrified the life out of me. What were the chances that all three brothers would pass away at the same age? They died in the same order they were born, too. It felt like some kind of sick, twisted Brothers Grimm fairy tale.

I was starting to feel that my life was being taken over by constant loss. Surely things would have to improve at some point. *There must be happiness out there for me*, I thought to myself. I am not making excuses for my affair, but I'm convinced that, as well as revenge, part of my reason for doing it was in the pursuit of any kind of happiness. I was terrified of being left on my own with two young children and a mental illness. What if I was on my own for the rest of my life? I'd always thrived on having people love me or want me. What else was there if I didn't have that in my life?

Peter eventually met another woman and started a life with her.

It was a very strange feeling. Deep down I knew I no longer had any feelings for him, but it was very odd seeing him build a life with someone else. And so I kicked off. I got angry. I said things I never should have said. I made his life hell for a little while. Why not? He'd done it to me.

Peter dealt with me so well – I can only imagine that it was because he was used to my slightly insane and aggressive behaviour. He encouraged me to be friends with him, for the sake of our kids if nothing else.

Miraculously, I was together enough to agree. We started spending more time together, even going out for a meal at one point. I even started to panic that I hadn't made the right choice and tried to reconcile things with him again. I was rebuffed.

'It's not going to work,' Peter said to me gently. 'We've tried too many times recently to fix things. It's not going to happen. Let's just concentrate on making this okay for the kids.'

I accepted this, but I was apprehensive. I really was by myself now. My affair had ended. Peter was gone. I was mentally unwell and had no idea what the hell was wrong with my brain. I knew then that I was in for a bumpy ride.

I tried my hardest to make life as happy as it could be, with continuous bouts of depression and psychosis. I rode out the hard times to the best of my ability. When my mind was clearer, I booked a holiday for me, Mam and the kids. I tried to keep up a friendship with Peter, asking him to come over and watch Peter Anthony and

Bernadette while I went out. But once the divorce was finalised we put a stop to it. It was too hard for us to continue like this.

At the start of the following year I had to take my beautiful little poodle Pepi to the vet. The poor thing was getting old now and clearly wasn't in a good way. He'd been staying with Peter for a while, as for some reason it was the only way he would settle down. I felt heartbroken enough as it was, but on the day Peter and I had a blazing row. It was a hard enough day to begin with, but I was incredibly stressed. I was reluctant to sign the papers giving permission for Pepi to be put down, and Peter kept pushing me to get it over with.

I know now that Peter wasn't being unreasonable. But I needed someone to blame for my anguish. It felt easier to drown out my grief with anger towards him. I accused him of being hard on me and refusing to show me any affection. As I said, I wasn't rational at this point.

During this time I felt constantly bombarded by illness. It felt like no sooner had I learnt to deal with one loss that I was hit with another. My heart ached constantly and I desperately sought a way to get rid of my pain.

I started to resent not having space alone with my kids. Mam was still living with me and wouldn't move back into her new bungalow, which was just around the corner. Since being released from hospital I'd occasionally been seeing a CPN again, and she recognised my resentment for what it was. She knew that the lack of space, coupled with all this stress and loss, was becoming too much for me.

'I really think you need to consider moving back into your own home,' she told Mam. 'Karen needs her space.'

I really appreciated this, but irritatingly Mam paid her no attention. She just didn't want to let go and I felt smothered and trapped.

The classic signs of my illness were returning and I felt like I was at rock bottom. I was angry at the entire world. When was I going to be allowed to become an independent woman and live my life for myself and my children? When was I going to be free from this constant barrage of mental illness? I knew myself enough by now to know that it was stress that made me so ill – each and every time.

All I wanted was to run away with Peter Anthony and Bernadette; I wanted to share my life with them and for us to have a little peace in our lives. Was that too much to ask for?

I reached breaking point. I packed a bag and kept the kids off school. I planned a couple of nights away – I can't even remember where, and I had no intention of telling anyone where, either. I went to the nearby Presbyterian church and told everyone I could that I was running away with my babies. Of course, I only meant to go for a short time, but I didn't tell them that. I didn't need to.

What business was it of theirs, anyway?

Before I had the chance to leave, the police turned up at the church. I found this mildly amusing until I realised that they were there for me. My friend had realised how poorly I was and had called them.

'I'm not coming with you,' I told them calmly, trying to tamp down my fury. But it made no difference. My community psychiatric nurse arranged for the kids to go back to school and told Mam I'd been admitted again. I was taken back to hospital.

This was beginning to feel old. The saddest part was that it could have been prevented. I'd known that I was becoming unwell again. I'd reached out and asked people for space, or asked them to make my life easier. And it hadn't happened.

Everyone needs time to get their head around various issues that are going on in their lives, but I wasn't granted that space. I also found it incredibly hurtful when I found out that my sister was helping my mam with the kids while I wasn't there. Deep down I couldn't help but wonder where everyone else had been when I needed that help.

Regardless of any of that, I was sick to the back teeth of being ill and not being able to understand myself. As God was my judge, I made up my mind that this was to be the last time I would ever darken the doorway of a mental hospital again. I was tired of putting everything else first before my own sanity and wellbeing. It was time to give a little attention to myself.

From now on, my own health was going to be of the utmost importance in my life.

CHAPTER 22
At Last, a Real Diagnosis!

So once again I found myself sitting in a mental institution, wondering where it had all gone wrong and how I could make sure that it never happened again.

This admission was scarier than previous ones. I had actually ended up on a locked ward. In my state of constant paranoia, it made for a horrific experience. The treatment wasn't tailored to our individual needs, and so I found myself in a ward where people of many different illnesses were stuck together.

This terrified me. Some of the others behaved in a way I couldn't understand. Sometimes there was a lot of noise, and sometimes people were deathly quiet. Sometimes people behaved in ways that I couldn't get my head around. Some had eating disorders, some had schizophrenia, others were dealing with severe depression. I knew they were different from me as we didn't display the same symptoms, which made me feel even more alone. If that was even possible.

My paranoia made my life extremely difficult. For me, it meant that I was never sure whether people were genuinely poorly or just acting. I am sure many would have asked the same question about me.

I often appealed the decision to section me. I also wanted answers. I wanted to know why I was becoming so poorly all the time and why it seemed to be happening every two years. Okay, so it was very apparent that there had always been a big, upsetting life event preceding my depressive states or psychotic episodes, but why did it always have to end this way for me? Was it ever possible to avoid or prevent hospitalisation?

I struggled when my family visited. I was so happy when I got to sit and play with little Peter Anthony and Bernadette, but I struggled whenever Mam turned up dressed for a night out. It hurt knowing that if she'd just agreed to give me some time to myself back at home, then this admission could well have been avoided. I also hated feeling like life was continuing on the outside without me. Was I really so unimportant that it barely affected anyone?

I asked questions all the time, but no one could really answer them. That was, at least, until the nurses told me to make a list of all the questions I need answering. I was then told to take them to the new psychiatrist.

That was the one thing about this stay that was more positive than the others. A new psychiatrist had come aboard. Perhaps I could put my trust in them and relate to them. It gave me a tiny ray of hope in an otherwise bleak existence.

There'd been so many times over the years when I'd been reluctant to take medication. Some of the ones that I'd been prescribed had been awful. As well as causing me massive weight gain, some of them made me feel drowsy and lethargic. At times I'd even spat them out in front of hospital staff. I was never interested in taking them for very long because the initial side effects were so horrific. I never had any real staying power with them.

But something in me had shifted now. Instead of fighting, or hiding from, the idea that I might have a serious, chronic illness, I started embracing it. I was prepared to admit that maybe I needed to face it, head on, in order to be able to understand it and beat it. I'd always been diagnosed with anxiety and depression, but I knew it was something more. It was time to get some knowledge without accepting any brush-offs. It was time to find out what my illness really was.

In the next ward round I asked my doctor, Dr Cornwall, the questions that I desperately needed answers to:

Why, no matter how many times I got better, did I always relapse again?

Why did my darkest days often involve psychotic episodes, hallucinations or delusions?

Why did I sometimes become aggressive and spend money recklessly?

Why did a lack of sleep trigger my symptoms?

Why did I often lack concentration and have racing thoughts, when I should have been paying attention to something?

Why did I sometimes engage in irresponsible behaviour?

Why did I often feel guilt and extreme bouts of sadness?

To his credit, my doctor took the time to listen to what I had to say, and answered my questions to the best of his ability. We talked for a while. Whenever I mentioned another symptom, he would nod his head as though confirming something in his mind.

I'd never really opened up like this to a doctor. I'd certainly never listed all of my problems, all in one go, like this before. I'd often been ashamed of some of the things I was now desperate to discuss.

At that point I knew I should have done this earlier – I should have admitted everything to the medical staff around me in the past – because when I'd finished, my doctor had a diagnosis for me.

I had bipolar disorder.

The term didn't mean an awful lot to me at first, as I'd never heard of the condition before. Thing like that weren't widely discussed back then, not in the way that they are now. But the doctor explained to me that I'd shown all the classic symptoms every time I'd become ill.

It always followed the same pattern: the lack of sleep, followed by episodes of mania, leading to depression. Often it was a deep depression.

I had first become ill in 1986, avoiding hospitalisation, and then there had been a gap until 1992. There were then further episodes in 1994, 1996, 1998, 2000, and now 2002. Only in 1994 had I avoided hospital admission, perhaps due to immediate intervention with medication. All of the other times I'd been admitted and sectioned for a number of weeks.

It was a very scary thought to think that this may go on for the rest of my life. But, I was reassured by Dr Cornwall, this didn't have to happen.

Over the next few weeks we had many discussions about my diagnosis. I told the psychiatrist about all of the losses I'd suffered throughout my life. I told him that I could sense my deceased family around me and that I knew they were sitting on my shoulder, guiding me.

As we'd discussed my bipolar tendencies at length, Dr Cornwall realised that I was entering a manic phase. I often became very focused on religion at this point, talking lots about God and the church. I also had bundles of energy. I couldn't sleep unless given medication. I would talk very fast, barely stopping for breath. After studying me for some time, the doctor knew that my mania would eventually calm down and that a depressive spell would follow it.

When you're bipolar and going through a manic phase, you look at life through rose-tinted glasses, and everything you see is great. So when you finally settle down, you become aware that life is not as marvellous as it appeared to be before. This causes you to become deeply depressed. With bipolar disorder, your mood can be very up and then very down, switching between the two very quickly.

Fortunately, my psychiatrist had a plan for rectifying my problem. I would always have bipolar disorder, but there was a way for me to start managing my bipolar brain in order to live life successfully. He would give me the tools to recognise my triggers and know what to do to stop the worst from occurring.

Of course, the severity of my illness meant that I had to be cooperative. And so, on Dr Cornwall's recommendation, I started taking medication again. After a short while, this allowed me to start having sensible, informative discussions with him about how we were going to tackle my mental illness. Without my cooperation, further hospital admissions couldn't be prevented.

I was about to embark on the road to recovery and start a plan that would change my life.

I cannot describe how grateful I felt just for being given a proper name for my illness. There was no need for me to deny anything, or block anything out of my mind, any longer. This was the first step to accepting that I could take control, if only I was willing to do so.

This also allowed me to come to terms with the fact that I might have to stay on medication, perhaps for the rest of my life, in order to stay well. I was determined by now, as there was just no way I ever going to leave my beautiful children again. It ripped me apart that I couldn't be with them, and that I had to watch others taking care of them for me. They were mine. They were my life. With them in mind, I would agree to anything to keep well.

As the weeks passed by, my therapy with Dr Cornwall continued. As I began to respond well to my medication, which was a godsend as now it was tailored to my illness, I started to feel stronger. I especially felt stronger when he started teaching me the tools to handle my thought processes at times of extreme stress and mood swings. I couldn't necessarily stop the onset of the various stages of my bipolar disorder, but I could learn how to control my unhelpful thinking patterns when they occurred.

During this time I had a little bit of home leave, but then I was asked to appear at my appeal for them to remove my section. I was so relieved to win the appeal. Technically it meant that I could just walk away and go home, but I didn't do that. Though it was difficult, the doctor asked me to wait until the weekend was over.

It was one of the longest weekends I've ever endured, but true to his promise he arrived on the ward to speak to me first thing on the Monday morning. He had a chat with the staff and then asked if he could speak with me.

I'd been prescribed a mood-stabilising drug and advised to carry on taking it indefinitely. He told me he would monitor me as an outpatient, but I needed to give him my full cooperation. Even if things were to get difficult, I had to stick with it and continue with my therapy sessions. I wasn't to give up putting in the hard work. I vowed to take whatever medication I had to, and to attend any and all appointments that were made for me.

I made myself a promise: no way was that hospital ever going to see me again. Of course being sectioned was nothing to be ashamed of; it never, ever is. But I'd had enough of living my life with a constant fear of going back. I had a life to live and that was what I intended to do. I now had something I'd never had before: awareness and acceptance.

It was up to me, now, to go out and search for brighter days. And if that meant accepting my bipolar brain for exactly was it was, then so be it.

CHAPTER 23
Light at the End of the Tunnel

This time at home, things were going to be very different. I was going to put me and my children first.

Previously I had allowed myself to be manipulated, but I hadn't realised that until now. Mam had always been very interested in what Peter and his new partner were up to, and I had stupidly allowed myself to be dragged into it. But my therapy and counselling had put life into a fresh perspective for me, and it had to stop. Now.

Although there were still issues regarding Peter Anthony and Bernadette that had to be resolved, it had to be done in a mature manner. This way, I could prevent and manage as much stress as was under my control. It was time for everybody to move on in their lives.

I definitely had to move on with mine.

I must admit that I am so grateful to Dr Cornwall. He helped me to see what was worth getting worked up about, and what wasn't worth the hassle. I knew I couldn't avoid stress wherever I went, but I could make the choice to create the healthiest environment for myself.

Mam carried on living with me, but I didn't intend it to be forever. I was still feeling a little vulnerable having just left hospital, and I suppose as things were calmer I was grateful for the company. But I knew that when the time came for me to ask her to leave and give me some space, I was strong enough to do it this time.

And so life went on. Mam and I did our best to enjoy our lives. We had the odd night out together and enjoyed the karaoke. I continued to try and inject as much positivity into my life as I could, to mitigate the sadness and stress.

Every time we went out socialising, we went out to our local. It wasn't until a friend of mine said that maybe we should try somewhere else that I realised I could really introduce some novelty back into my life again.

'You'll never find a new man in your life if you keep going in there,' she laughed. 'It'll only happen when you finally make the move and look elsewhere.'

I chuckled along, but to be honest romance was the last thing on my mind. I'd had enough heartache and misery to last a hundred lifetimes, and I'd only just managed to understand myself properly, let alone anyone else. If anything like that was to happen, I would do the usual Karen thing and let fate decide. I was too busy trying to control my mind without trying to control my romantic life as well.

I was now approaching my 35th birthday and Mam and I had made plans to take Peter Anthony and Bernadette to Whitby to celebrate. I had also booked to take them on a little overnight trip to London with a coach holiday. I felt fantastic. My confidence was back where it belonged. And just by chance, Mam and I heard about a karaoke night in Middlesbrough. What the hell, we thought. It was my 35th birthday. Why not give it a try?

I will never forget the weather that night. It started absolutely bouncing down with rain; I had never seen rain like it. But it wasn't going to stop us from going out; my birthday was as good an excuse as any to put on some smart clothes. I seemed to live in jeans at that time and I wanted to feel confident again. I put on some nice black trousers, with a lovely floaty top, and my high heels. I felt amazing.

We had been at the pub for over an hour, singing and giggling away, when Mam pointed out a man who was sitting at the bar.

'He keeps turning around and glancing over at you,' she said.

I giggled. 'I'll check him out when I go to the bar for drinks. Don't keep looking at him!' I blushed like a teenager. I hadn't felt like this in a long time.

When I went up to get our next round of drinks, I did my best to subtly check him out. I was very impressed with what I saw. He had a lovely head of thick dark hair, with little flecks of grey. He looked very smart, in dark trousers and a striped shirt. And, though I didn't normally like them, he was sporting a moustache that suited him very well. A little while later, I became aware that he'd moved over to the other side of the bar, closer to where Mam and I were sitting. We kept giving each other fleeting glances. *Look into My Eyes* by Bryan Adams was playing in the background. It was all very romantic.

Later that evening, as we were about to leave, he followed me. At first he pretended that he was on his way to the toilet, but then he asked me if I'd be there the next week. I said I was – well, I was now!

The following week, when we returned to the pub, was to be a turning point in my life. Paul, as I found out his name was, asked me for my phone number before I left. And it was the beginning of something special.

I didn't want to jump right in, though, without being absolutely sure that it wouldn't cause me a load of grief to get involved with him. We talked and talked and talked on the phone, sharing personal stories and getting to know each other. So far so good. But it was what he revealed next that really surprised me.

'Things aren't easy at the minute, Karen,' Paul confessed to me. 'My mum's in the hospital. She had a breakdown recently. Thankfully she's recovering somewhere safe right now.'

This really took me aback. I didn't expect him to tell me something so similar to my own story. It encouraged me to be open and upfront about mine.

He'd shared so much sensitive information with me, I had no hesitation in sharing a little of my illness and my history. One or two of my mam's male friends were later horrified to find out that I'd disclosed this information before we'd even met up. But I couldn't have cared less about their views. After all, if Paul had any issues with this, it was better I knew from the start, as there was no way I could live a lie any more. I had this illness and it wasn't going anywhere soon. I suppose I trusted my instinct and realised that he was far too caring to pass judgement on me.

Thank God he was incredibly understanding. It didn't put him off at all – soon we had our first date at the pictures, followed by our first night away together in Whitby, and he was even better looking now that he'd shaved off his moustache! From our very first date we became pretty much inseparable.

We'd both been quite lonely for a while until then. We were both divorced and had gone on to have destructive flings or relationships afterwards. But we both knew, from day one, that our relationship was going to be something special. It was a massive help to know that Paul had raised his children on his own for some time, as sadly they had lost their mum. I knew that it couldn't have been easy for a man to do that on his own. It takes a special kind of strength for anyone to be able to do it. It meant that he'd be likely to be great with my own kids.

Our relationship progressed very quickly, but I tried my best to make sure I knew what I was getting into. I wanted to know that I was making the right decision, but deep down I knew it was for keeps.

I am not in any way suggesting that it has all been plain sailing. As with all second marriages, there can be many obstacles to overcome. We certainly had our fair share of battles when friends or family members had some issues adjusting. But the important thing is that when you've found something so good, you try so hard to keep it that way. Paul and I were engaged soon after we met – believe it or not, on that beautiful bridge in Kincasslagh, Donegal. And no, in case anyone is wondering, there was no Daniel O'Donnell present! We were married in May 2007.

My last admission to hospital was in 2002, touch wood. I say touch wood, as I never take my recovery for granted. I continue to take my medication, which is an anti-epileptic drug. This sounds strange, but actually it really does work.

The important thing for me to say is that I still see my psychiatrist, and I have a new community psychiatric nurse who I also see regularly. But medical professionals can only give us the tools – it's down to us as to how we use them in order to stay well.

I may have avoided hospital since then, but it doesn't mean I don't have to monitor my illness. I'll never be free from it. But what's different is how I tackle my issues when I'm faced with them. In the past few years I've faced stigma, judgement, and oppression. As mentally ill people we will always come across this – at least until we normalise it for good.

My life will never be what it was before the illness started, but what I do have now is insight. And trust me, insight is one of the most valuable things you can have when you're bipolar.

The new Karen doesn't run away from stress. She doesn't deny its existence. She doesn't try to avoid dealing with her issues. Instead, she looks at them and says, 'How can I deal with this in the most effective way possible?'

One of the most valuable methods I have is to learn to recognise what triggers my manic and depressive episodes. I then take whatever steps I can to take a step back.

Sometimes it's taking the extra medication I have on standby, which helps me rectify my sleep patterns and slows my brain down. But more importantly I listen to myself. What is my mind telling me I need? Do I need space? Do I need quietness? Do I need to ask for a bit of extra help to get me through a rough patch? Can anyone help me look after the kids, or just sit down with me and reflect on what makes me feel good in life? Never underestimate the value of listening to yourself and acting on your own intuition.

I've also learnt to try not to be scared when I can feel a relapse coming. Bipolar disorder is with me for life; there'll be times when I won't feel great. But if I can slow my breathing, control my panic, and be open and honest with those around me, I can stop the bad times becoming overwhelming.

That's not to say that I handle things perfectly. A few years ago, I had to embark on twenty-two weeks of cognitive analytical therapy to help me to get things back on track.

I was haunted by sad memories from my childhood, to the point where I was crying all the time. I tormented myself with guilt, telling myself that I'd not always been there enough for Mam. But counselling helped me to see that the needs I had as a child were being met now by my husband and my children. And more than that, it helped me to see that I didn't need anyone's approval in order to be the best person I could be. I was valuable with or without other people's validation. It helped me see all the positive things I had in my life right now.

I worked hard in therapy. And that's the reason it was of such great help. Therapy only works when hard work is put in by both sides.

It's all very well wanting to be well. But do you want to *work* towards being well?

CHAPTER 24
My Lightbulb Moment

As the years went by, I constantly looked back and tried to work out the things that triggered my illness.

But it wasn't until one of my visits to my therapist that I heard one word – one word which identified the root of my personal illness: conflict.

When the occupational health doctor asked me why I thought I often became ill, I would list the many specific situations that caused my decline. But he helped me to see that there was a running theme throughout a lot of them. And that was conflict.

Surely enough, when I looked at what had happened to me recently, it made sense. There'd been a lot of conflict in my most recent workplace – the social services – and that had caused me to become poorly again.

I also started to look back over the times when I had lost sleep or suffered a sharp relapse, and the answer was often the same: my problem was with conflict.

It goes without saying that we can't live in a perfect world where there is no conflict. Therefore, all that I can do to protect myself is to try to foresee possible conflict and stay away from it. As time went by in my last job, I realised that my work situation was never going to get any better, and in the end I decided that the best option would be for me to resign. I made this decision for myself, no one else. I wasn't exactly in the best financial position to be able to just leave work, but in the end it came to the choice of going to work for the money and becoming ill, or leaving and being well in myself. I wanted to be happy, so I chose the latter. Here was a perfect example of how I could take control of my life and my triggers.

I don't want to make things sound like my life has been a bed of roses since being diagnosed. I've still had many issues to contend with. Eighteen months ago, Mam became so poorly that she had to go into a care home. This was actually what caused me to walk away from my job. As I had access to her records, I was able to check that the correct information about her was being recorded.

Sadly, this led to me facing a disciplinary hearing and, despite never having done anything of this nature before in my entire career, my employer gave me a final warning. They said I'd breached confidentiality and deemed my actions as gross misconduct.

I just couldn't cope with the stress of the conflict. I felt it painted me in the wrong light, as I'd always respected everyone's confidentiality. For me, this was different: Mam was an eighty-four-year-old lady who only had me in the world to look out for her. But they didn't see it this way, and I couldn't handle it. Therefore, I felt I had no option but to resign from my post, before my bipolar really made things terrible for me.

I never imagined in a million years that Mam would go into a care home. She was always such a strong woman. Over the years she's joked with me, saying 'Don't ever let me go into a care home, especially if I start forgetting who you are. If I ever say "Who are you?" then that's me finished.'

The sad irony of this is that is exactly how life is now turning out. I knew things were going wrong some time ago, when Mam stopped going out and kept falling over. She kept being taken into hospital, which again caused my stress levels to spike. But I had to remember that it wasn't about me this time: it was about her. I fought for a long time to get Mam the care she needed, the kind of care that I could no longer provide for her myself.

Things finally came to a head when she had a terrible fall while Paul and I were visiting her. Thankfully, we were there to help her straight away, as the outcome could have been tragic. When she fell, the emergency pendant that she wore around her neck didn't trigger an alarm. After she'd spent a couple of weeks in hospital, we realised that she couldn't live on her own again.

The day I had to empty her bungalow and rehouse her two little poodles, which she'd adopted from me some years ago for company, broke my heart. I knew it was the right thing to do, but as you know by now, loss never affected me very well. Mam tried her best to persuade us to take her home, but we couldn't. It was hard for me too. I had made her bungalow so lovely for her with new carpets, furniture, ornaments and other decorations, only to find a couple of months later that we had to let it all go.

It actually felt like a kind of bereavement, even though Mam was still alive. It was like the Mam I knew and loved was being taken away from me. She was no longer there for a cuppa and a quick chat any more. Our regular six o'clock phone call no longer happened. I now had to accept that life was changing and that my future visits to Mam would be in the care home. It was a true test of all I'd learnt in my cognitive analytical therapy: I had to reprogram my thinking so that loss didn't trigger a manic or depressive episode. It wasn't easy; it took a lot of work to keep control of my bipolar brain.

I knew at this point what I had to do to remain emotionally and mentally strong. So I made sure that I got plenty of sleep and allowed myself to be supported by my family. I tried my best not to shoulder too much of the burden.

As my family constantly reassured me, we had done the right thing by Mam by getting her the support that she needed. I had to remind myself of that fact. Mam loved her new home, and for over a year she could genuinely recognise the benefits of being there.

Sadly, I now faced having to deal with a diagnosis she was given just over a year ago – Alzheimer's and vascular dementia. For a long time I thought we could keep this at bay with regular visits, lots of talking, and looking at photos. But that can only do so much. Mam is deteriorating quickly and in the space of two weeks she suddenly lost touch with reality. She has forgotten that Dad has died and believes he is still alive and has girlfriends.

It's very bizarre being on the opposite side of such unfortunate beliefs or delusions.

Once upon a very difficult time, I would never have thought that I'd be able to handle a situation like this. I'd have been convinced that I'd go down the same road that I always have, and become ill again with the stress of it all. But I'm determined not to do it this time.

I have all the support I need around me, and for that I'm very grateful. I'm also well aware that it's down to me to keep on top of my therapy, my cognitive tools, and my thinking patterns in order to remain strong. And that's what I intend to do.

It's worth saying that even if I don't succeed, that's okay too. I'm only human, and there'll be some dark days. I will just move forward taking one day at a time, just like everyone else, as that is all any of us can do. The difference now is that I feel equipped enough to tackle it.

I do love Mam so much, but equally I am a mam myself and I don't want my children to see me poorly if I can help it. I will continue to search for those brighter days, and so far it's working. Bipolar disorder is not who I am – it's a mental illness, and it doesn't have to control me.

CHAPTER 25
How I Cope Now

Having a diagnosis for my illness meant that I had to finally accept it was never going to go away. And that was okay.

I have been learning, and continue to learn, how to manage my bipolar disorder. And for me, that's been a real turning point. I can already feel the difference in my quality of life. Never underestimate the power of understanding yourself and your own mind. I would advise anyone who's worried that they might be bipolar to seek a diagnosis as soon as you can. It doesn't have to get as bad for you as it did for me.

One big turning point for me was when I found a consultant who was prepared to listen to me. Only then could he give me the right diagnosis, the right medication, and the right therapy.

In the past I was prescribed medication that was totally unsuitable for me. It would make me fall asleep and not want to face the world. I tried to tell the previous consultant that it wasn't helping me at all, but he had no interest in listening to me. I was always given the impression that he felt I was reluctant to take my tablets, but that wasn't the case. I just wanted to have a proper life!

That's why it's vital to find someone who is willing to listen. And please don't give up if your experiences are negative to begin with –

my story proves that if you keep trying, eventually someone will listen to you. Someone will help you.

Dr Cornwall realised that I wasn't simply refusing medication. I just didn't want to spend my entire life in bed. He was the one who prescribed sodium valproate to me. This is the tablet that is often taken by people who have epilepsy. Please don't take this to mean that this is the right medication for you – your doctor should always determine that. Apparently mine isn't common in the treatment of bipolar, or at least it wasn't at the time, but he had his reasons for thinking that it would work for me. And so I was prepared to give it a go.

As I had been extremely poorly, he gave me a fairly high dosage to begin with. I was prepared to accept that the tablets might take some getting used to. At that point, I was prepared to do anything that would stop me from having to return to hospital.

When I began the medication I had regular outpatient appointments with the doctor. He made me feel protected and confident. There are always some side effects with tablets, especially when you're new to them. The main one with these were that the tablet caused constant hunger pangs, which only a lot of food could take away.

This might sound like something I had no control over, but actually my therapy taught me that I could tackle this problem too. I started ensuring that the food I ate was healthy. I did still gain a hefty amount of weight as I'd gone from running around manic and not eating during my manic episodes, to being calm and tired. But although it bothered me a bit, it was still more important that it helped me get mentally well. I could deal with the weight at a stage when I felt I could tackle it.

As I saw my doctor on a regular basis, he constantly asked me if I felt the tablets were working and if I had any issues with them. As time went by and he adjusted my dosage to the right level, he suggested that I might find it easier to take my tablets in the evening. That way, I wouldn't feel the hunger pangs as I would be asleep. Sure enough, as long as I had a little sandwich or something with them, they worked and by morning I didn't feel the need to eat. It helped me a great deal.

There was only one occasion when things went wrong, when I felt that I might become very ill again. Things were going so well with my medication that the consultant and I had gradually reduced the dosage. I was very keen to see whether it would be possible to be medication free one day.

We decided that, seeing as though it'd been a while since I'd been ill and I was only taking a small dosage, it was worth attempting to come off them all together. It wasn't a decision we took lightly, and I never would have done it without my consultant's approval.

Everything went fine for a few weeks. But then there was a bit of a bust up between me, Susan and Mam. I felt like I was stuck in the middle of it all. Unfortunately it ended in a huge family disagreement and, in true Karen style, I started to blame myself. It was that typical bipolar guilt kicking in again.

True to form my sleeping pattern became disrupted again. And as I wasn't taking my medication, this time there was no safety net for me. I started to fixate on the disagreement, thinking of little else. Very soon my mind started to race again. I tried to watch TV and, like all those years ago, I'd get through a programme without acknowledging any of it. I was far too preoccupied.

The following day, after Paul had gone to work, I felt a very strange feeling creep over me. I sat in my bedroom, staring at a box of paracetamol tablets. I didn't know why I was doing this. I didn't want to end my life.

Immediately I rang my consultant. I left a message for him to ring me as soon as possible. I then rang my GP as I was becoming more and more distressed. I had to convince the receptionist that it was vital I saw the doctor as a matter of urgency. It took a while to convince her that it was a true emergency.

Eventually she made an appointment for me to see the GP that afternoon at 3pm. God, that amount of time seemed like an eternity. I didn't know if I could trust myself or my actions. I rang Paul and he wanted to leave work and come rushing home, but I persuaded him that he didn't need to. I'd made all the necessary appointments and had rang a taxi to take me to Mam's. I knew I'd feel safe there, as she'd seen me in this state before. She'd be able to watch over me until it was time for me to see the doctor. I promised Paul I would ring him as soon as I reached Mam's, but I guess I didn't realise just how much I'd panicked him by announcing to him how I was feeling. He must have felt petrified.

The consultant returned my call when I was at Mam's. I became more and more upset.

'Will I end up back in hospital?' I wailed, certain that this now made me a failure. 'Will I go back to hospital, doctor?'

That was my worst fear. I'd vowed to myself that I'd never go back there. He could hear how distressed I was, but he couldn't promise me that I wouldn't be sectioned again. He didn't know how fast things would escalate.

'Let me come off the phone with you, Karen,' he advised me. 'I'll call your doctor and tell him the medication you need to get you back on track.'

I nodded to myself, tears rolling down my cheeks. 'I'll take whatever you want me to in order to get better,' I promised him. I think I was really promising myself.

When I put the phone down, I realised Paul had been trying to get through to me. He was all set to come over to Mam's, worried that I'd not made it. I managed to tell him that I was perfectly safe with Mam and wouldn't do anything silly. We agreed for him to collect me and take me for my afternoon GP appointment.

That day was one of the longest of my life. I did nothing but watch the clock until it was time to see the doctor. I was so relieved when Paul collected me and we were on our way. I couldn't wait to get my tablets and feel well again. The doctor gave me the prescription and after collecting the tablets I went home to bed. I took a tablet before I went to sleep.

Bernadette somehow sensed that things weren't quite right. She was almost a teenager now, and very astute. In an attempt to slow me down, she suggested we played a game on her laptop which involved virtual driving. As unusual as it sounds, it ended up being a great distraction. As I focused on the game, my thoughts slowed down and my mind stopped racing. I did my best to have fun, as it feels almost impossible to have a good hearty laugh when you're having a 'wobble', as I explained it to Bernadette.

I slept exceptionally well that evening and was very groggy the next day. My mind was already starting to calm down. Over the weekend I began to feel like the old me again. I was taking sodium valproate again at a higher dosage.

First thing on Monday morning, I had an appointment with another consultant, as mine was away on holiday. He was very patronising. He couldn't understand how I could possibly be feeling better so quickly. But Paul spoke up for me; he'd witnessed the transformation for himself.

It had to be the fastest turnaround I'd ever had. It opened my eyes even more to the fact that insight, awareness and tailored treatment is the best thing for my illness. It proved to me that I, personally, needed the medication. If I'd stayed on it, I might have been able to cope with a little bit of conflict. The tablets kept me on an even keel.

I also knew, then, that I needed to remain in the mental health medical system at least for a while longer. My consultant knew me best and knew what was required to make me well again.

The difference between me and the old Karen is that I can now recognise that things like this are just 'wobbles'. They will always happen, but now I'm equipped to deal with them. I can take ownership of my bipolar disorder. I can manage my illness and lead a fruitful life.

In the spirit of this, I later decided that I needed to tackle the weight that I'd gained during my trauma, and embark on a fitness routine like I had done a few years before. Only this time, I wouldn't become obsessive over it. Although it was a struggle, I soon came to realise that the most important benefit of the exercise wasn't my weight at all: it was how great I felt afterwards. That little rush of endorphins after a workout did absolute wonders for my mental health. It sounds so simple now, but you'd be amazed how much it helps.

The weight wasn't going to drop off, but I was feeling good. I knew that this was the best way forward. From then on, I have always managed to do some form of exercise – be it fast walking, swimming or keep fit classes. If I become bored of one, then I simply switch to another.

I can honestly say that keeping fit has seriously helped me in the last few days. I won't allow myself to give up my activities. There may be days when I literally have to drag myself off to a swimming pool or spinning class, but I know that once I'm there I'll really enjoy it. And most importantly, I'll feel better about myself in so many ways. Not only does it help my mood, but it's been a massive boost for my self-esteem. And as low confidence is an obvious trigger for me, I'm clearly onto a winner. It's taken me years to tone up and lose the weight I gained when I was ill, but I've genuinely loved the journey.

Along with keeping fit, I have continued, and hopefully always, continue, to see my doctor as an outpatient. Just because I've regulated my medication, that doesn't mean that the illness is sorted and I'll always be fine. That's simply not true. Managing life with bipolar disorder is a constant battle.

Here's how things usually go for me: slowly I begin to notice that things aren't quite right. I will go to bed and not be able to sleep. This doesn't always ring alarm bells for most people, as it's fairly common in today's hectic world. But when I can't sleep, usually it's because there are too many thoughts that go flying around in my mind.

For example, when I used to work, I would lie awake at night having conversations in my mind, trying to think of ways to resolve a particular conflict. The next morning the situation would not seem anywhere near as bad, but the previous evening it would be the most important matter in the world. And as anyone who suffers insomnia will know, night time is a very lonely time. When one of those nights turns into two or three, that's when I start to panic.

The doctor reassured me that just because I'm losing sleep, that doesn't mean I'll always have another episode. But as I was still very worried about the impact of sleeplessness, we decided to put in place a back-up plan.

The doctor gave me a course of olanzapine tablets, which are a kind of relaxant. They are specifically tailored to bipolar disorder and they help to straighten out my mind, preventing delusions. If I ever got too worried and sleep eluded me, I could take one and it would help me sleep. I was relieved to find that it worked perfectly, and often found that I may only need them for one or two nights to rectify my sleep pattern. I do my best to keep this kind of thing to a minimum, though. I don't want to become too dependent on drug-induced sleep, but it's good to know that there's a safety net.

Being taken care of by a great medical team is so comforting. But I must remember that they can't do all of the work for me. I constantly remind myself of the word 'intervention'. I have to keep working hard to manage my bipolar disorder. If I, myself, am not aware that something is going wrong, then no one else can help me. If I ignore any signs that my illness is creeping in, then it can have disastrous consequences. When it gets hold of me, it can spiral within a day or two, and by that point no one can tell me I'm poorly. By that point I'm too far gone to compute this.

And so in this way, I'm in control of my own mental health. It's been a huge learning curve for me, but now I can look out for my triggers and I can spot the warning signs. I can then deliberately change my pattern of thinking, and the environment around me, to make my mind work for me, not against me.

This is why going for so many years without a proper diagnosis proved disastrous for me so many times. I urge you to seek out a diagnosis if you have any concerns like I did. That way, people can help you take control of your mental health like I did with mine.

They can help you find that lightbulb moment.

CHAPTER 26
Searching for Brighter Days

I know I'll still have sad days ahead of me. We all do. But my life is so well balanced now, in comparison with the darkest days of my illness.

Meeting my husband was a huge, positive turning point in my life. No relationship is free of ups and downs, but as the years go on you learn how to compromise with each other. Much like I've had to compromise with my bipolar brain.

I don't think it's easy being married to someone who has bipolar, as I can be extremely jealous and very sensitive. But I'm also one of the most loving, caring people you could ever ask to meet. And so I feel that, for those reasons, I'm worth putting up with! I'm so grateful that I have support, and a good family network has been vital for my wellbeing.

Life has become so much easier as my children have got older. They were always a massive support for me, even from a very young age. I miss their childhood a lot as we did have a lot of fun, but I can appreciate them in a whole new light now that they're young adults. I know that they'll always have my back. They'll always look out for me. I am their mother but they're also my best friends.

One of the most vital pieces of advice that I can give you is to always make time for yourself, whether it's time to read a magazine, keep fit, or whatever helps you unwind. Because we are all in need of some 'me time' sometimes – and I've learnt that the hard way so that you don't have to. I live for my nights away with my husband, my holidays, and even just a couple of glasses of wine at a weekend.

I have a new little pooch, Bonnie, who helps me more than you'd think. I find that dogs are very in tune with how we are feeling, and mine is a massive support when I'm feeling low. They can also make you more active – a dog always needs a walk, and getting out there in the fresh air, meeting people, is yet another effective tonic for mental illness.

Over the years I have also become aware of just how important it is to maintain friendships where you can. Social interaction is a natural part of human life. My girlfriends offer me a lot of support and inject a bit of positivity into my life. It is lovely to be able to meet for a coffee or a bottle of wine every now and again, just to put the world to rights. So thanks so much to Jane and Jude, my two besties!

These things are all part of my coping mechanism and help me to keep well, but you will have your own. Maybe mine will provide some inspiration for you if you're feeling a little lost.

Never be afraid to reach out if life starts getting hard. There is never any shame in asking for help. It's not always easy to get, but I promise you that help is out there.

I admit that I wept a bit for all the precious time I lost to bipolar disorder. But there's no sense in looking backwards now.

For so many years I constantly searched for brighter days. Now, finally, I've been able to find them.

ACKNOWLEDGEMENTS

Thanks to my wonderful son and daughter, Peter and Bernadette, who have always supported me throughout my journey and given me a reason to battle my illness. I would also like to thank my wonderful husband Paul for continuing to stand by me through some difficult times. You all show me unconditional love and I feel truly blessed to have you all in my life.

I must also thank my editors Kasim and Stephanie – you helped me tell my story and for that I am grateful!

the *Shaw* mind
FOUNDATION

Supporting children, adults and families
for better mental health. **#lets**do**stuff**

Sign up to our charity, The Shaw Mind Foundation
www.shawmindfoundation.org
and keep in touch with us; we would love to hear from you.

*We aim to bring to an end the suffering and despair caused
by mental health issues. Our goal is to make help and support
available for every single person in society, from all walks of life.
We will never stop offering hope. These are our promises.*